SUSAN WATKINS

# Jane Austen's Town and Country Style

*With 177 illustrations, 77 in colour*

*Special photography by*
*Hugh Palmer*

*RIZZOLI*
NEW YORK

*To Sid, my husband, for his love, support,*
*guidance and criticism;*
*to our children Matthew and Anthony for their*
*patience and enthusiasm, and to Sid,*
*Jessica, Alistair and Martha, whose individual*
*achievements have inspired me.*

On the half-title page: *Attractive English printed cottons and*
*chintzes of the late eighteenth and early nineteenth centuries make*
*their appearance in this patchwork quilt sewn by Jane and Mrs*
*Austen in 1811.*

Frontispiece: *A standard Georgian sash window, given a*
*Gothic treatment fashionable in 1809, when Jane Austen's brother*
*Edward had the window cut into the drawing room of Chawton*
*Cottage, Hampshire, offering the occupants garden views of*
*flowers and fruit trees divided by gravel walks.*

First published in the United States of America in 1990 by
Rizzoli International Publications, Inc.
300 Park Avenue South, New York, NY 10010

Copyright © 1990 Susan Watkins
Layout © 1990 Thames and Hudson Ltd, London

Library of Congress Cataloging-in-Publication Data

Watkins, Susan
  Jane Austen's town and country style / Susan Watkins.
    p.   cm.
  ISBN 0-8478-1232-4
  1. Austen, Jane. 1775-1817—Contemporary England. 2. England–
–Social life and customs—19th century. 3. England—Social life and
customs—18th century. 4. Manners and customs in literature.
5. Decoration and ornament—England. 6. Interior decoration–
–England. 7. City and town life—England. 8. Country life–
–England. I. Title.
PR4038.E46W38   1990
823'.7—dc20
                                                          90-52602
                                                          CIP

Printed and bound in Singapore

# Contents

# Preface

I N these pages, from the vantage point of a particular English country gentlewoman, a journey is made through the society and surroundings of a group of people of unsurpassed elegance and refinement, in the later decades of the eighteenth century and at the beginning of an era of profound change that followed it. *Jane Austen's Town and Country Style* offers an opportunity to wander, to gaze and to gain an almost tactile understanding of this world – the world of Jane Austen.

Here we will see *how* the country gentry lived – in an ambience of cultivated politeness, with a keen though delicate sensibility, well balanced by common sense – as well as how they dressed and dressed up, dined and feasted, performed and were entertained, in a selection of social settings.

We will also see *where* they lived, the aesthetic perfection of the English country house crowning an almost equally perfect landscape. The interior designs of the rooms, complete with colour, texture and appointment of furniture, are rendered from visual impressions in the novels supported by personal and historical archives, and then reconstructed to create an imaginary model of Mansfield Park.

Mansfield Park is a good place from which to consider a central question – did Jane Austen draw her characters and settings from actual experience? But this book is not about the structure of Jane Austen's novels and her characterizations; nor is it an examination of the chronological details of her life. These subjects have passed time and time again through the sieve of expert analysis.

The perspective – appropriate to a lady of rank – is confined to the personal and social life of the men, women and children of the upper classes, and their circle of domestic interests. Far from being bland, this presents the sublime world of southern England's great houses, the socially competitive atmosphere of London's elegant drawing rooms and Bath's assembly rooms, as well as the robust attractions of the period's most popular coastal resorts. It is a perspective that tends to overlook the era's

Above: *Panel from a classically inspired chiaroscuro wallpaper frieze, from Warren Hastings' Daylesford House in Gloucestershire. Hastings was a long-standing friend of the Austen family.* Opposite: *Detail from an early nineteenth-century French wallpaper, possibly from designs by Vernet (1758–1836), used during the present century to decorate the main bedroom at Godmersham Park, the Kent country seat of Edward Austen Knight.*

more unsavoury aspects – disease, squalor, social injustice; but as Jane herself said, 'Let other pens dwell on guilt and misery. I quit such odious subjects as soon as I can.' (*Mansfield Park*)

During a period when Haydn was composing, and Turner and Constable painting, English domestic architecture was enjoying its Golden Age. Within the environment of Jane Austen, as depicted through her novels, the country house and its landscaped setting are chronicled as an enduring achievement, harmoniously linking classical order and nature. The doors are then flung open to reveal the shade and stripe of wallpaper, the pattern of chintzes and rugs, and the arrangement of expertly designed and crafted furniture. The book invites the reader to be a surreptitious onlooker in another time through a frozen-frame sequence of rooms, their fashionable occupants stilled in mid-motion. In the drawing room we can eavesdrop on detailed observations of the cut and design of costume, as well as the occupation of looking one's best. In the dining room, a display of food and drink, on the age's best china, plate and crystal, is unobtrusively admired, and menus considered, while appetizing smells drift up from the kitchen.

We can no longer live to the full the beauty, balance, dignity, grace and manner that are thus displayed; but by seeking to blow away the mist that has accumulated over the years since Jane Austen wrote her novels, and to look with clarity into her society and surroundings, we may discover customs, artistic appreciation and visual styles – from textile patterns to interior design – that retain their validity even today.

*This simple pedestal table is believed to have been Jane Austen's writing table. It was here, near the window in Chawton Cottage, that she liked to work in the mornings after breakfast. Opposite:* Educated ladies purchasing reading matter from Lackington's bookshop in Finsbury Square, London, 1809.

I · A Society of
Grace and Manners

HOUGH JANE AUSTEN'S knowledge of the world reached far beyond the relative confines of a country parson's unmarried daughter, her distinctive awareness of life and the vagaries of society began with the country parson himself, the Learned Reverend George Austen. Born in Kent, he was a descendant of an honourable family of clothiers known as the Grey Coats of Kent. The family owned two small manor houses in the sixteenth century, gradually building up their holdings over the next two centuries and making some members substantial landowners. But misfortune and the inheritance laws diverted the family's wealth away from George Austen's father, William Austen, so that George began life in less than genteel circumstances. William Austen then earned his living as a surgeon in Tonbridge, Kent, at a time when medical men were considered among the menial strata of society. He married a widow, Rebecca Walter, who already had a son, William Hampson Walter. William and Rebecca Austen had four children together, three of whom survived: Philadelphia, George and Leonora. Of the last-named, little is known, except that she was all her life dependent on the charity of relations and died a spinster. George's mother died soon after the birth of her last child, and his father remarried but left him an orphan when he was six. His stepmother took little interest in him, and it required the benevolence of George's wealthy lawyer uncle, Francis Austen of Sevenoaks, to see to his needs and to pay for the boy's education at Tonbridge School, where his academic achievements led him to St John's College, Oxford, on an Open Scholarship. In 1754 he left Oxford to become the curate at Shipbourne and in 1755 a master at Tonbridge School, but he returned to Oxford in 1758 as a Fellow of St John's and assistant chaplain of the college. He was a proficient scholar, well read in several languages and with a developed appreciation for literature that encompassed a broad range of literary styles. He was pleasant-natured, handsome, and generally at ease with society. Perhaps it was his intellectual and social attributes, combined with good looks – he was popularly known as 'the handsome proctor' while a Don at Oxford – that first aroused the notice of the Master of Balliol's niece, Cassandra Leigh.

Jane Austen's mother, Cassandra, was the daughter of the Reverend Thomas Leigh, rector of Harpsden near Henley-on-Thames in Oxfordshire and known as 'Chick Leigh' for his rapid success in being elected a Fellow of All Souls' College. Although Oxford, academia and the clergy provided some common ground to link George and Cassandra, Mrs Austen's forebears were considerably more exalted than her husband's. Her great-uncle was the first Duke of Chandos – a noble title, though perhaps not a noble character, for his ostentatious lifestyle was much criticized. Another of her ancestors, Sir Thomas Leigh, had been Lord Mayor of

*James (1765–1819), the eldest of the Austens' six sons, was devoted to literature and poetry. Although most gentlemen of this period were 'dropping in' to verse, James had more talent for it than most. Jane (right) was to become the more famous writer of the family, however. The silhouette (far right) probably shows her only sister, Cassandra (1773–1845), to whom the author remained particularly close throughout her life.*

London under Queen Elizabeth I, and his son had sheltered Charles I at Stoneleigh Abbey in Warwickshire in 1642 during the Civil Wars. The stately, aristocratic Stoneleigh Abbey became the family seat of the Leighs of Adlestrop in Gloucestershire, to which Cassandra belonged. Cassandra was the namesake of her great-aunt, the Duchess of Chandos.

The Reverend Austen took holy orders in 1760 and married Cassandra Leigh at Walcot Church in Bath in 1764. Before his marriage, George Austen was presented with the living of the parish of Steventon, near Basingstoke in Hampshire, of which his cousin Thomas Knight was the patron. Thomas Knight was a wealthy landowner with large property holdings in Kent and Hampshire and two imposing mansions, Godmersham Park and Chawton Manor House. To the Steventon benefice Francis Austen of Sevenoaks added the neighbouring living of Deane, thereby providing the thirty-three-year-old clergyman with enough security to begin married life. The Austens first settled in Deane, accompanied by Cassandra's mother and the motherless seven-year-old son of Warren Hastings, future governor-general of India. Hastings probably committed his son to the care of the rector on the recommendation of George Austen's elder sister, Philadelphia Hancock, the wife of Dr Tysoe Saul Hancock, an English surgeon working in India, where the couple had become close friends of the governor-general. Equally, Hastings had been friends with Mrs Austen's relations, the Leighs, since his childhood in Gloucestershire. The Reverend and his wife were therefore known to him, and he could be confident of his son's security and upbringing. Young Hastings was a sickly child and only lived another three years, which caused Mrs Austen as much grief as if he had been her own child – the Austens' kind affection was long after remembered with gratitude by the boy's father. Happily, the Austens began to have sons of their own. James was born in 1765, followed by George in 1766 – a mentally defective child about whom little is known – and Edward in 1767. A few years later the Austens moved to the rectory at Steventon, which saw the birth of Henry Thomas in 1771, of the first daughter, Cassandra Elizabeth, in 1773, of Francis William in 1774, Jane in 1775 and the last child, Charles John, in

*Edward Austen is presented to Mr and Mrs Thomas Knight, his adoptive parents, by his father, the Reverend George Austen.*

1779. Added to the Austens' growing family were the pupils that the schoolmaster Reverend Austen took in to supplement his income.

The rectory came with a small farm, on which the Reverend Austen produced wheat, harvested with the aid of his bailiff, John Bond. Mrs Austen, in addition to looking after her eight children, superintended the kitchen garden and flocks of chickens and ducks, while keeping a watchful eye on the dairy maid and on the cook's baking and brewing. From their mother Jane and Cassandra began to learn the crafts of the gentlewoman: needlework, art, music and managing a large household. From their father they gained an appreciation of scholarship. The Reverend Austen, with his unusually large library of over five hundred books, brought them history, geography and literature – even Gothic intrigue – by encouraging his children to read, often aloud, as an evening's amusement within the family circle, and to discuss freely what they had read. The pleasures of the written word even extended to their own composition. For the most part, the girls received their education at home, though there were two brief episodes of formal education. The first was with a Mrs Crawley in Oxford in 1782, when Cassandra was about ten and Jane seven. Mrs Austen had intended to send only Cassandra, thinking Jane still too young. But 'If Cassandra were going to have her head cut off, Jane would insist on sharing her fate', said Mrs Austen; thus the two little girls, together with their cousin Jane Cooper, went off to Oxford. The following year Mrs Crawley removed her small school to Southampton, where her establishment was besieged by 'putrid sore throat', and Jane nearly died. Jane Cooper wrote to her mother of the potential tragedy, and Mrs Cooper and Mrs Austen immediately removed the girls. The second and last school at which the Austen girls were educated was the Abbey School in Reading, where they stayed until 1786 or 1787.

The Austen boys James and Henry were also educated by their father until they were old enough to go to Oxford, where James, the true scholar among the children, extolled the ideals and virtues of a poet while airing his nationalistic Tory views as editor of a journal called *The Loiterer*. James, like his father, became a clergyman and eventually succeeded to the living of Steventon, among others. Henry also wrote for *The Loiterer* while at Oxford, but his nature was more carefree than his brother's, and his career more eventful; he was in turn a captain in the Oxford Militia, a temporarily successful London banker, receiver-general for Oxfordshire, a bankrupt and a clergyman.

Francis, a year older than Jane, and Charles, the baby of the family, were educated at home until they were fourteen and twelve years old, respectively, when they went off to the Royal Naval Academy at Portsmouth. Both had very successful naval careers during one of the most heroic, albeit unruly, periods of British naval history. Both brothers became admirals; Francis received a knighthood, the much-coveted Order of the Bath, and Charles retired as commander-in-chief on the North American and West Indies station.

Edward, Jane's third eldest brother, had an education and upbringing of a much different pattern. Mr and Mrs Thomas Knight, the son and daughter-in-law of the Reverend Austen's distant relative and patron, developed an affection for young Edward, inviting him to stay at their mansion in nearby Chawton, and later for extended visits to Godmersham Park in Kent. These visits became longer and longer, so that the boy's father began to worry that Edward was getting distressingly behind in his Latin grammar. But the visits increased, and the Knights eventually proposed adopting Edward, then in his teens, making him heir to their estates. It was not unusual for families to perpetuate ownership through distant relations in this way. Realizing the enormous advantages in this arrangement for their son, the Austens agreed, but in spite of the separation, Edward remained close to his natural parents, brothers and sisters. Edward's education was then expanded to include tutelage in the management of vast landholdings and country estates, as well as in the art of being a polished, articulate gentleman with a gentleman's cultural sensitivity. For the latter aspect of his studies it was necessary to embark on a grand tour of Europe, to acquire a connoisseur's appreciation of Roman ruins and Renaissance architecture. Edward must have found this phase of his education to be worthwhile, because he was later to send his own sons on a grand tour. Upon receiving his inheritance in 1812, Edward Austen became Edward Austen Knight. (For the sake of continuity I have used the name Edward Austen Knight throughout, regardless of the date.)

For Jane Austen, the focal point of her world was her family, a perspective expanded and made highly colourful through the varied and successful careers of her brothers, news of which was brought home by the family's continuous correspondence. More importantly, she acquired first-hand experience of life beyond her Hampshire village – bolder, with more lustre and with human nature more capricious – for the most part through numerous extended stays with her brothers and other relatives. During long visits with Henry and his chic wife Eliza, Jane developed an acquaintance with London, the capital of fashion and good taste, in its public manifestations – the theatre, concerts, art exhibitions, pleasure gardens and smart West End shops, patronized by the haughty elegants of select society – and in the private 'make or break' social soirées of the city's genteel drawing rooms. At Godmersham Park, the Kent country seat of Edward Austen Knight, Jane delighted in an existence of pure leisurely comfort maintained by an army of servants. Amid the sprawling Palladian splendours of Edward's mansion, with its six hundred acres of exquisitely landscaped parkland, she enjoyed Godmersham's illustrious visitors and gracious dinner parties, as well as being entertained by the neighbouring family at Chilham Castle and making overnight stays at the stately Goodnestone Park, home of Edward's in-laws, the family of Sir Brook Bridges.

## *The world beyond*

The British were at war for most of Jane Austen's forty-two years (1775–1817). During the year of her birth English soldiers were engaged in the American War of Independence, which lasted until their defeat at Yorktown, Virginia, in 1781, though the war did not officially end until the signing of the Treaty of Paris in 1783. The years 1789 to 1799 were those of the French Revolution, which electrified the English upper classes with a mixture of horror and satisfaction. Between 1812 and 1814 Britain was again at war with America, overlapping the country's fight against France and Napoleon, which began in 1793 and ended with the Battle of Waterloo two years before Jane's death. While England's shores were under threat of invasion from France, the southern coastal resorts were populated with men in uniform, as was the capital. People living in rural areas were kept aware of the country's war efforts through the newspapers' running commentary on naval exploits and battles, making war heroes the idols of the nation. With two brothers fighting in Nelson's navy, the events of war became more personal.

Even the startling incidents of Revolutionary France directly touched the Austen family – brought to Steventon in the form of Eliza, daughter of Mrs Philadelphia Hancock. Dr Hancock had brought his wife and daughter to England from India in 1765. In 1769 it became necessary for Dr Hancock to return to India to earn more money, but in 1775 he quietly died there, never to see his wife and child again. During those years Mrs Hancock and her daughter Eliza spent a great deal of time with the Austens at Steventon, forming an increasingly strong attachment to the family. It had been the Hancocks' desire to educate their daughter in Europe, so when her husband died, Mrs Hancock went to live abroad, eventually settling in Paris, where Eliza grew up amidst the glitter of fashionable Parisian society. In 1781, at the age of nineteen, Eliza the coquette married Jean Gabriel Capotte, Comte de Feuillide: 'he literally adores me', she wrote to her cousin Philadelphia Walter, and is 'entirely devoted to me ... making my inclinations the guide to all his actions'. In 1786, expecting a child, she left for England, where her son was born. She named the baby Hastings after her godfather, Warren Hastings.

In England Madame la Comtesse de Feuillide was received at Court – her slight frame bedecked in voluminous stiff satin, stretched over the wide side-hoops of ladies' Court dress, in which she was obliged to stand for two hours. She returned to France from time to time, but was always eager to get back to England and the fashionable company of London, Tunbridge Wells and the coastal resorts. She also made time for extended visits to Steventon, where she enthralled her cousins with detailed accounts of French society.

The history of the effervescent Eliza then entered a darker phase. In 1791 her mother died, and the Comte left behind a mistress in order to come to England and comfort his wife, taking her to Bath for a bit of gaiety. On the couple's return to London they were met with letters announcing that if the Comte de Feuillide did not return to France immediately he would be declared an émigré and have his estates confiscated. Perhaps not realizing the danger provoked by his royalist associations, and needing to rescue what little remained of his fortune, Eliza's husband returned to France. In 1794 the Comte de Feuillide, like Robespierre, was executed on the guillotine a year after the commencement of the Reign of Terror.

The widow Eliza never lacked male admirers; James and Henry Austen became particularly ardent suitors. James was the first of the brothers to propose marriage to his cousin, but was refused; the life of a Hampshire clergyman was probably too bucolic for Eliza. Henry, nine years her junior and a captain in the Oxford Militia, was accepted, though not without considerable wooing. She had once described him as being taller than his father, a characteristic that apparently met with her approval, and she admired his powdered head, dressed 'in a very *tonish* style'. The couple were married in 1797, when Jane was twenty-two years old.

It was ten years earlier, in 1787, that Eliza had joined the Austens at Steventon in their Christmas theatricals. Keen amateur actors, they sometimes put on their plays in the dining room of the rectory, but this year a full house was expected – in both the domestic and theatrical sense – and the large barn in a meadow near the rectory was required to seat the expected visitors. Eliza had seen *Bon Ton* by Garrick and Mrs Cowley's *Which is the Man?* during a recent visit to Tunbridge Wells, and was anxious that she and her cousins adapt them for a performance in the barn theatre; but the young Austens had other ideas and enticed Eliza into joining them in a risqué play called *The Wonder! A Woman Keeps a Secret* by Mrs Centlivre. Twelve-year-old Jane was no doubt dazzled by the addition of this fascinating cousin to the family circle.

*A scene from David Garrick's comedy* Bon Ton, or High Life Below Stairs, *first performed at Drury Lane in 1775. Eliza wanted to adapt the play for a performance in the Austens' barn theatre in Steventon.* Opposite: *The trial of Warren Hastings, which opened with spectacular public ceremony in 1788, aroused great controversy and excitement in social circles.* Inset: *Sir Joshua Reynolds, who had painted this portrait of Hastings 1766–8, was among those who attended sessions of the trial.*

The year 1787 also marked an event that may initially have been of only minor interest to the budding teenager, but it was an incident much discussed in the rectory, and provided dazzle of a different nature: the beginning of impeachment proceedings against the politically powerful Warren Hastings, Eliza's benevolent godfather, friend of the Austen family and a favourite with King George III. The charges against Hastings – 'High Crimes and Misdemeanours', involving corruption and plunder during his term of office as governor-general of India – were brought forward in a speech to the House of Commons given by the dramatist and Whig MP Richard Brinsley Sheridan. So movingly eloquent was the speech that Sheridan was offered a thousand pounds for the copyright within twenty-four hours of having spoken it, and it was described twenty years later as the finest speech that had been delivered within living memory of man. The trial, which was to last seven years, was begun in 1788 with a parade of spectacular royal, civil and military ceremony. During the proceedings the galleries were thronged with some of the era's most notable figures, encompassing the queen and her daughters, Mrs Fitzwilliam, to whom the Prince was secretly betrothed, the political hostess the Duchess of Devonshire, portrait artist Sir Joshua Reynolds, the composer Haydn, the novelist Fanny Burney, scientists, historians, poets and the cream of society. They were brought to a fever of uncontrollable emotion when Sheridan delivered his rapturous orations: 'Handkerchiefs were pulled out; smelling-bottles were handed round; hysterical sobs and screams were heard; and Mrs Sheridan was carried out in a fit' (*Macaulay's Essays*, vol. 3, London, 1895).

At length, in the spring of 1795, Hastings was absolved of his crimes, being solemnly called to the Bar, where the Lords acquitted him. He

bowed, then respectfully retired. The furore of public interest had waned over the years, but towards the end was once again aroused to celebrate Hastings' victory. Hastings withdrew to Daylesford, his country seat in Gloucestershire, but again claimed public attention in 1813, when he was called to the Bar as a witness on Indian affairs. His esteem reached Oxford University, which conferred on him the degree of Doctor of Law, and in the Sheldonian Theatre 'The undergraduates welcomed him with tumultuous cheering'. Soon after, Hastings was sworn into the Privy Council and admitted to a lengthy private audience with the Prince Regent; when the emperor of Russia and the king of Prussia visited England, Hastings appeared in their train. In 1813, in a letter to her sister Cassandra, Jane Austen wrote, 'I long to have you hear Mr. H.'s opinion of P. and P. His admiring my Elizabeth so much is particularly welcome to me.' Hastings' old adversary, Sheridan, was also an admirer of *Pride and Prejudice*, recommending that a Miss Shirreff buy it immediately, for it was one of the cleverest things he had read. Warren Hastings died in 1818, just over a year after Jane Austen's death.

Remarkably, there was a second trial and ensuing public scandal of concern to the Reverend Austen's family. In 1799 Mrs Leigh-Perrot, the wife of Mrs Austen's brother, was arrested and charged with stealing a card of white lace from a milliner's shop in Bath. The value of the lace was high enough to categorize her offence as a capital crime, which usually demanded death by hanging if found guilty or, more likely in this instance, exile in Botany Bay. The proud Mrs Leigh-Perrot was imprisoned for eight months before her case came to trial, during which time Mrs Austen, who felt sympathy for her sister-in-law, offered Jane and Cassandra as companions to cheer the woman while she was in gaol; but the offer was refused. At her trial, which opened on 27 March 1800, before a courtroom of two thousand persons, Mrs Leigh-Perrot was allowed to make a brief statement in her own defence. Her words were few, but carried great emotion. It took the jury less than ten minutes to decide upon her innocence. During the same assize, five of Mrs Leigh-Perrot's fellow prisoners were sentenced to death; among them was a fourteeen-year-old burglar.

## *The education of a lady of rank*

The rich, eventful life of Jane Austen, intermingled with the trappings of her brothers' success, the drama of war, the taint of public scandal, and played out against the enormous social upheaval of the Industrial Revolution, is scarcely detectable in the novels, but her knack of acute observation, practised in an expanded array of social circumstances and settings, could not but enhance the mood, texture and perspective of her writing. What is clear, is that her perspective, however heightened, never exceeds the conventional boundaries of the society in which she moved, and remains that of a lady.

'Her eloquent blood spoke through her modest cheek', wrote Henry Austen of his sister; 'Her voice was sweet; she delivered herself with fluency and precision; indeed she was formed for eloquent and rational society, excelling in conversation as much as in composition'. These qualities were acquired in part through her early formal education, but more through the contents of her father's bookshelves and her lifelong appetite for reading. As the eighteenth century progressed, the art of conversation, based on a knowledge of history, literature and poetry, was increasingly nurtured as a suitable accomplishment for ladies. Gentlewomen, now well versed in such topics, were expected to be companions to their male counterparts, where previously their role had generally been that of decorative adjunct and housekeeper. 'I declare after all there is no enjoyment like reading!' said Miss Bingley in the hope of attracting Mr Darcy's attention and approval; 'How much sooner one tires of any thing than of a book! – When I have a house of my own, I shall be miserable if I have not an excellent library' (*Pride and Prejudice*). In 1791 the bookseller James Lackington commented: 'There are some thousands of women who frequent my shop, that know as well what books to choose, and are as well acquainted with works of taste and genius, as any gentleman in the kingdom, notwithstanding they sneer against novel readers.'

Although novel-reading was considered by many a wanton and even dangerous pastime, Mrs Radcliffe's Gothic novel *The Mysteries of Udolpho* (1794) – satirized by Jane Austen in *Northanger Abbey* – achieved widespread popularity well into the nineteenth century. Novels of morals and manners, such as the works of Maria Edgeworth and Fanny Burney, were more to Jane's taste; indeed, she appears to have taken the title of her own novel *Pride and Prejudice* from the last two pages of Miss Burney's *Cecilia*. Another favourite with Jane, and the rest of the nation, was Scott's first novel, *Waverley*, published in 1814, which achieved overnight success.

The crowded bookshelves of Steventon Rectory provided the Austens with great diversity of literary taste: the novels of Fielding, Richardson and Smollett were in company with the works of Shakespeare, Dr Johnson, Goldsmith's *History of England*, Sherlock's *Sermons* and Blair's *Rhetoric*. An essay on the *Military Police*, Thomas Gisborne's *Enquiry into the Duties of the Female Sex* and Charlotte Lennon's *The Female Quixote, or the Adventures of Isabella* were also available to Jane.

Henry Austen said that his sister had been, from an early age, enamoured of 'Gilpin on the Picturesque', meaning the works of the Reverend William Gilpin, a popular scenic writer and illustrator whose essays fuelled the craze for both appreciating and creating the emotive beauties of a 'Picturesque Landscape'. In *Pride and Prejudice* the heroine Elizabeth Bennet travels north, plotting a route similar to that taken by Gilpin dur-

*Amongst the volumes ladies might have selected in Lackington's bookshop were novels of contemporary morals and manners by Fanny Burney – who was much admired by Jane Austen – and Gothic romances, such as* The Mysteries of Udolpho *(left) by Mrs Ann Radcliffe, which was satirized in* Northanger Abbey.

ing his travels, and in *Mansfield Park* Mr Rushworth plans to engage the services of the famous landscape gardener Humphry Repton, to contrive a natural chiaroscuro arrangement of his scenery. A sensitivity to nature was also developed within the Austen family when, in the early evenings following their dinner, the rector read aloud the poetical works of Cowper. Marianne Dashwood of *Sense and Sensibility* despises Edward Ferrars for his inability to be 'animated' by the poet.

The education of the daughters of society's upper echelons was begun at home with a governess; the Miss Bertrams (*Mansfield Park*) knew of Asia Minor, could put the map of Europe together and name the principal rivers in Russia. Other young ladies, like Jane and Cassandra, learned by devouring their father's library. A period of home study – reading and discussion – was usually followed by a few years away at school, where the major emphasis was on dancing, dress and deportment. At the Abbey School near Reading, Jane and Cassandra went to 'speeches and playacting' at the nearby boys' school, and the boys in turn were invited to join in dances at the Abbey ballroom. Jane and Cassandra were also taught smatterings of French and Italian at the Abbey School, as well as history, spelling and the necessary needlework. But the most memorable subjects appear to have been the Abbey's ghosts and the artificial cork leg of the headmistress. At Mrs Goddard's school in *Emma*, 'a real, honest, old-fashioned boarding-school', Harriet Smith received 'a reasonable quantity of accomplishments at a reasonable price'; it was not an institution 'where young ladies for enormous pay might be screwed out of health and into vanity'.

*Although most young ladies of the period were taught at home by a governess, several select establishments existed for their education. The young brother in George Morland's* A Visit to the Boarding School – *happy to see his sister again – would still have been under the tutelage of the governess.*

*Dancing was considered an essential accomplishment for all young ladies of quality. In this engraving from* Le Bon Genre, *a dancing master accompanies his pupils on the violin; one studies her pose in a mirror, while another maintains her balance with the aid of a chair.*

For learning how to budget personal and household accounts, *The Young Ladies' New Guide to Arithmetic* by John Grieg (1803) was the answer, 'being a short and useful Selection, containing besides the common and necessary Rules, the application of each Rule, by a Variety of Practical Questions, Chiefly on Domestic Affairs; together with the Method of Making out Bills of Parcels, Book-debts, Receipts, Promisory Notes, and Bills of Exchange; also a variety of useful tables'. The book was recommended for use in 'Ladies' Schools' and by 'Private Teachers', and though 'More particularly intended for the "Use of Young Ladies"', it was 'Equally useful as an Introductory Book for the Junior Pupils of Gentlemen's Schools'.

In the eighteenth century it was customary for a young lady to complete her education by working a sampler, embroidered on a woollen cloth called a 'tammy'. Henry Tilney told Catherine Morland, 'I had entered on my studies at Oxford, while you were a good little girl working your sampler at home!' (*Northanger Abbey*). Embroidery on silk tinted with watercolours was the evidence of Charlotte Palmer's expensive education (*Sense and Sensibility*): in her bedroom there 'still hung a landscape in coloured silks of her performance in proof of her having spent seven years at a great school in town to some effect', while Mrs Goddard's parlour in *Emma* was 'hung round with fancy-work'.

Jane Austen enjoyed needlework of all kinds; 'we are very busy making Edward's shirts', she wrote to her sister in 1796, 'and I am proud to say that I am the neatest worker of the party'. Her more intricate work included a shawl that she made for Cassandra, with a satin-stitch design embroidered on muslin, and a white lawn handkerchief embroidered with a variety of motifs. In 1811 the three Austen ladies combined their efforts to produce a patchwork quilt of coloured chintz; 'Have you remembered to collect pieces for the Patchwork?' Jane asked Cassandra. 'We are now at a stand still.' Needlework was one of the few accomplishments that a gentlewoman could pursue with equal vigour after marriage. In the novels, most of the female characters spend part of each day at needlework. Lady Bertram in *Mansfield Park* 'spent her days in sitting nicely dressed on a sofa, doing some long piece of needlework, of little use and no beauty.' Lady Bertram had also done a great deal of carpet-work, while Mrs Jennings (*Sense and Sensibility*) busied herself in making a rug. Embroidery worked on a tambour frame was another popular needlecraft of the eighteenth and nineteenth centuries. The technique involved passing a fine hook through fabric to create a series of chain stitches. Mrs Grant's tambour frame is mentioned in *Mansfield Park*, and in *Northanger Abbey* Catherine Morland gives some anxious consideration to her tamboured muslin dress.

The late eighteenth century and early nineteenth century found young gentlewomen earnestly engaged in two other drawing room accomplishments: art and music. Female amateur artists preferred watercolour over oils, the former becoming the more fashionable medium of artistic expression, dispensed in tidy little bricks of colour, which replaced messy powders. Drawing classes abounded, and the craft gave private employment to scores of spare drawing masters. While there was still some interest in portraiture, there was more enthusiasm for reproducing picturesque landscapes, so that a young lady never travelled without her box of watercolours. Cassandra Austen was a proficient watercolourist; in her teens she illustrated her young sister's mocking *History of England*, while her later watercolours are mostly of family and friends. A portrait of Laurence Sterne's Maria (1808) is thought to be among her best works. Other artistic pastimes included draughtsmanship, sculpturing in wax, paper-cutting, shellwork, japanning (a hard black lacquer used on wood or metal then decorated with gilt), and modest attempts at furniture-making; Mr Darcy's sister drafted a 'beautiful little design for a table' (*Pride and Prejudice*).

Mr Darcy's sister also played the harp, as did Mary Crawford, in *La Belle Assemblée* style, in the drawing room of the rectory in *Mansfield Park*; and as too did Fanny Austen Knight, Jane's favourite niece, the daughter of her brother Edward, in her Uncle Henry's drawing room in London. But the keyboard was the traditional musical instrument of ladies, and the introduction of the piano forte in 1758, a forerunner of the 'upright', placed this instrument in all the country's best drawing rooms. For the discerning musician, the works of the masters – Haydn, Handel, Mozart, Beethoven – were either available, being created or transcribed in this era of great musical composition. Jane Austen's personal collection of music included varied vocal works, some of them purchased, but most copied out by hand: Haydn, Handel, Giordani, along with Italian and French songs, settings of folk songs, popular ballads, songs from the pleasure gardens, comic songs and selections from operas. Jane managed to find time to practise on her piano forte every day; not so Elizabeth Bennet (*Pride and Prejudice*): 'My fingers', said Elizabeth, 'do not move over this instrument in the masterly manner which I see so many women's do. They have not the same force or rapidity, and do not produce the same expression. But then I have always supposed it to be my own fault – because I would not take the trouble of practising...'. The novels' champions of female ac-

*Though she was not especially fond of listening to music, Jane Austen, like many of her female characters, took her piano-playing seriously, and made time to practise every day. It was into these music books that she copied much of her music by hand.*

complishments are the two Dashwood sisters, Elinor and Marianne (*Sense and Sensibility*), who fill their days with useful reading, with drawing and painting for Elinor, and music for Marianne, all practised and perfected.

Although women claimed to practise these skills for the sake of self-improvement, it cannot be denied that, for some, the chief aim in being accomplished was to attract the notice of a suitable partner in marriage. A young lady could appear to advantage while gracefully fingering a keyboard, as a potential candidate held a candle over her music and turned the pages. But just as some women were choosing to become more selective in their reading, there were those who were genuinely striving for perfection in their other talents, aspiring to the level of a virtuoso on the keyboard, of a master of art, or even sculpture.

The real test for the talents of a well-bred young lady took place after she had 'come out'. To 'come out' was to make a formal entrance into society upon reaching womanhood. The time of entry varied; in some families, if an older sister was 'out' but not yet betrothed, younger daughters might be kept back until their older sisters' prospects were more in hand. In *Mansfield Park* Mary Crawford expresses some confusion over Fanny Price's arrangement with society: 'Pray, is she out, or is she not? – I am puzzled. – She dined at the Parsonage, with the rest of you, which seemed like being *out*: and yet she says so little that I can hardly suppose she *is*.' The training for becoming at ease amongst society took place during the 'season' in London or Bath, where young ladies took in, and were seen at, the theatre, concerts, exhibitions, balls and other gatherings. A successful season was crowned with marriage.

# *Marriage – with or without love*

Marriage was a matter of concern to the whole family, for not only was a daughter's, or even son's, financial future decided upon becoming betrothed, but also the security of unmarried sisters – and perhaps the bride's mother, if widowed. Family ties were binding; brothers- and sisters-in-law were simply 'brother' and 'sister', and relationships with cousins and other distant relatives were much closer than they are today. Indeed, a person was known and given a place in society in accordance with the family with which he or she merged through marriage.

In the matter of marriage, young people were expected to consider their parents' wishes. Responsible parents placed enormous importance on money. Potential suitors were all the more eligible and attractive if, like Mr Darcy, they had an income of £10,000 per year. Mr Bingley, 'a young man of large fortune' resident at Netherfield Park, was Mrs Bennet's suitor of choice. '"If I can but see one of my daughters happily settled at Netherfield", she said to her husband, "and all the others equally well married, I shall have nothing to wish for"' (*Pride and Prejudice*). Several of the gentlemen in the novels are assessed as to their position in the marriage stakes according to the amount of their income and property. And female characters are similarly judged: Catherine Morland is forced to flee Northanger Abbey when General Tilney discovers that she has no fortune to offer his son; Mr Knightley sizes up Harriet Smith's prospects: 'What are Harriet Smith's claims, either of birth, nature, or education, to any connection higher than Robert Martin [a farmer]? She is the natural daughter of nobody knows whom, with probably no settled provision at all – . . . I felt that, as to fortune, in all probability he might do much better; and that as to a rational companion or useful helpmate, he could not do worse.' To be concerned about money was to be practical, and it was an issue continually met with during this period of massive inflation caused by the Revolutionary war with France. The war increased the fortunes of many, while obliterating others. A stable continuity of wealth was more likely when money married money – the most desirable arrangement, as with Miss Woodhouse and Mr Knightley. If love was also present, the result was pure harmony. Men of stature, but dwindling fortunes, sought to revive their estates by marrying women of fortune, though possibly of a lower social rank. This kind of emotional practicality is expressed by Charlotte Lucas in *Pride and Prejudice*: 'Without thinking highly either of men or of matrimony, marriage had always been her object; it was the only honourable provision for well-educated young women of small fortune, and however uncertain of giving happiness, must be their pleasantest preservative from want.'

Ladies without money or prospects had very few options. Professional employment was not open to women; the stage was unthinkable, and in the case of women such as Jane Austen, who earned money from writing, the earnings were either insufficient or too variable to be relied upon. Jane Fairfax (*Emma*) unhappily contemplates her future as a governess, while others in straightened circumstances considered becoming companions to elderly dowagers; in the absence of her fortuitous marriage Fanny Price might well have been in this position (*Mansfield Park*).

A formal proposal of marriage was addressed in a letter. Elizabeth Bennet, hearing that her father has received a letter, wonders whether Mr Darcy has made an offer for her hand, and is 'undetermined whether most to be pleased that he explained himself at all, or offended that this letter was not rather addressed to herself'. Fanny Austen Knight received a touching letter of proposal from Sir Edward Knatchbull: 'Dear Miss Knight – Much as I flatter myself that a favourable reception will be given to this communication; it is quite impossible for me to conceal the anxiety with which I shall await your reply.' Miss Knight's acceptance was given 'through the medium' of her father's pen due to the agitated state of her spirits, though she was 'fully sensible of the honourable Distinction shown her as well as the handsome and flattering terms' in which the offer was contained.

Years before, in November 1814, Jane had counselled young Fanny on another romance involving John Pemberton Plumtre, a young gentleman and scholar who was in line to receive a sizeable inheritance. Having encouraged the attentions of the young man, Fanny became indifferent upon being secure of his feelings: a perplexing state of affairs. The anxious girl wrote to her aunt, appealing for advice. In order to keep such a sensitive communication secret, Fanny concealed her letter in a parcel of music, which her unsuspecting father delivered to Jane on his visit to Chawton. Aunt Jane's advice was to consider the 'sterling worth of such a young Man & the desirableness of your growing in love with him again.' This was a position over which Fanny had already brooded; in order to excite her own feelings for Mr Plumtre she had visited his room, but on catching sight of his dirty shaving rag, her struggling sentiment was dashed to pieces. 'There *are* such beings in the World', wrote Aunt Jane,

> perhaps, one in a Thousand, as the Creature You and I should think perfection, Where Grace & Spirit are united to Worth, where the Manners are equal to the Heart & Understanding, but such a person may not come in your way, or if he does, he may not be the eldest son of a Man of Fortune, the Brother of your particular friend, & belonging to your own County.

The argument in favour of the match with Plumtre was then reversed, and Jane counselled 'I . . . entreat you not to commit yourself farther, & not to think of accepting him unless you really do like him. Anything is to be preferred or endured rather than marrying without Affection'. At the end of the following year an entry in Fanny's diary concluded: 'infidelity tending neatly to dispel all intimacy between the Plumtre family & myself'. Fanny's marriage to Sir Edward Knatchbull, which took place on 24 October 1820, appears to have been a happy one, for they had several children, including the first Lord Brabourne.

**Jane's** early nineteenth-century chinoiserie work cabinet, decorated with black lacquer and gilt, is fitted with boxes for storing needles, thread and sundry other items essential to the needlewoman; the workbag is underneath. In the background hangs the colourful patchwork created by Jane and her mother. Cassandra Austen's intimate study of Jane's favourite niece, Fanny Austen Knight (right), portrays her engaged in the delicate art of watercolours, a skill that Cassandra herself practised to a high level. Needlework was another highly prized skill, and most young girls of the period would have been expected to stitch a sampler like the one below – reputed to have been by Cassandra – as part of their general education.

Jane's advice to Fanny was probably heart-felt, in view of her own romantic experiences, which encompassed such emotions as hope and tragic disappointment. While Jane Austen's youthful behaviour has been described as flirtatious, it is generally believed that on only one occasion did she fall deeply in love. The object of this serious attachment was a young clergyman whom she met during the summer of 1801, while the Austen family were on a tour of Devonshire. Years later Cassandra is said to have remembered him as 'one of the most charming persons she had ever known', and the family apparently encouraged the development of the relationship, for they invited him to join them at a later stage on their tour. But instead of his arrival, a letter was received announcing his death. In November 1802 Jane's hand, if not her heart, became temporarily engaged with a proposal of marriage received from Harris Bigg-Wither. Although he was six years her junior, he was the brother of Elizabeth, Catherine and Alethea Bigg, close friends of Jane since her childhood at Steventon, and he was heir to Manydown, an impressive estate that would have secured not only Jane's future, but that of her sister and mother. After accepting his offer, overnight ruminations caused her to reverse her decision on the following morning.

Following a formal offer of marriage and its acceptance, the negotiations of the marriage settlement were begun. Miss Maria Ward brought 'only £7,000 to the marriage that raised her to the rank of a Baronet's Lady with all the comforts and consequences of a handsome house and large income' (*Mansfield Park*). Mr John Dashwood in *Sense and Sensibility* added to his own wealth by marriage. The 'settlement on the Intended Marriage of Edward Austen Esquire' in 1791 was contained in a massive legal document: to Thomas Knight (Edward's adoptive father) went various lands and rents for his lifetime; Elizabeth Bridges received £2000, which was to be invested. The ancient legal vernacular of the document went on to describe additional transfers of property, and the whole was signed by Thomas Knight, Edward Austen, Elizabeth Bridges, Fanny Bridges (Elizabeth's mother), as well as by Elizabeth's brother and uncles. (Sir Brook Bridges had died earlier in the year, hence the absence of his name.)

Marriages were by banns, or by licence from the bishop; a licence was more expensive. 'And a special licence. You must and shall be married by a special licence', said Mrs Bennet in *Pride and Prejudice*, such was the measure of her delight at the prospect of her daughter Elizabeth's marriage to Mr Darcy. Divorce was next to impossible. Only a husband – a wealthy husband – could obtain a divorce, and even then it required an Act of Parliament. Mr Rushworth in *Mansfield Park*, scandalized when his wife goes off with Henry Crawford, 'was released from the engagement to be mortified and unhappy till some other pretty girl could attract him to matrimony again, and he might set forward on the second, and it is to be hoped, more prosperous trial of the state.'

Although the preliminaries to a wedding were somewhat elaborate, the actual ceremony was comparatively restrained. 'The old fashion of festivity and publicity had gone by, and was universally condemned as showing the great bad taste of all former generations', wrote Jane Austen's niece Caroline Austen. The wedding of Caroline's half-sister Anna (their father was James Austen, eldest son of the Reverend and Mrs Austen) to Benjamin Lefroy 'was the order of the day': between nine and ten on a cold November morning, the bridal party, consisting of the couples' immediate families, departed from the bride's home for the church – the ladies in carriages, and the gentlemen on foot. The groom's father, a clergyman, read the service to the small congregation, and James Austen gave his daughter away. The party then returned to the bride's home for breakfast: 'The breakfast was such as best breakfasts then were: some variety of bread, hot rolls, buttered toast, tongue or ham and eggs. The addition of chocolate at one end of the table, and the wedding cake in the middle, marked the speciality of the day.' Soon after breakfast the bride and groom departed for their home in Hendon. Later that day at Chawton Great House, as it was called by the Austens, Captain Austen and his family, together with the newly arrived family of James Austen, no doubt drank the customary toast to the new couple. In the evening 'the servants had punch and cake.'

The wedding of Fanny Austen Knight and Sir Edward Knatchbull was similarly conducted, though Sir Edward and Lady Knatchbull departed from the church for their home, Mersham-le-Hatch, immediately following the ceremony. Charlotte Lucas and Mr Collins (*Pride and Prejudice*) also left directly from the church door. The honeymoon had not yet become customary, and it was not at all unusual for the bride to take along a sister or some other female relative with her to the couple's new home. Maria in *Mansfield Park* takes her sister with her, and in *Sense and Sensibility* Mrs Jennings blames Lucy Steele for being so unkind as to leave her sister behind when she marries Robert Ferrars.

*Love in a Window, etching by John Kay, 1787.*

# The daily round of a country gentlewoman

Once married, most ladies of rank and fortune found numerous interests to occupy the day. Upon awakening, a lady might drink cocoa, brought to the bedside by her personal maid, who would shortly dress and coiffure her lady for the morning. During the interval before breakfast – served at ten o'clock – there was perhaps time to begin the day's letter-writing, maintaining the communication of domestic events and minutiae between family members, relatives and friends. The writing and receiving of letters was an important part of the daily routine for all ladies, married or not. 'I have now attained the true art of letter-writing,' wrote Jane in 1801, 'which we are always told, is to express on paper exactly what one would say to the same person by word of mouth.'

The London postal system came into existence during the late seventeenth century, and until 1801 letters were picked up and delivered four to eight times daily for the price of one penny. The year 1794 saw the introduction of mail coaches to replace post-boys; these coaches, protected by armed guards, operated to strict schedules and were exempt from tolls. The Penny Post became the Twopenny Post in 1805, and by 1812 the cost of a letter was four pence for 15 miles or less, rising to seventeen pence for 700 miles; postage was paid by the recipient. The charge was based on let-

*The keyboard was the traditional musical instrument of choice for gentlewomen, and Haydn's visits to England between 1791 and 1795 ensured that his piano sonatas would have been included in the repertoire of most young ladies of fashionable taste.* Opposite: *Here are simplicity and comfort of a kind that could not have failed to appeal to Jane – a well-stocked bookcase, a folding writing desk with compartments for paper, pens and ink, and a view of the orderly garden.*

ters of a single sheet – more paper meant more money – and because of the cost, letters were usually written on a single page, which was then folded to make a small rectangular envelope and sealed with a wafer of wax. To save money, Jane Fairfax 'fills the whole paper then crosses half', which means that she wrote at right-angles across the first lines of writing (*Emma*). While it was a delight for ladies to keep up a correspondence with relatives and friends, it was thought improprietous for an unmarried woman to write to a gentleman unless she was engaged to him.

Either before or after breakfast ladies dealt with household accounts; this might include a discussion with the housekeeper or cook. It was also a time for reviewing menus and perhaps the preparations for receiving guests. Household business was not necessarily a daily occupation – it might occur weekly or monthly – but it always included the studious recording of accounts in a bound ledger. The Georgians liked writing of all kinds: poetry, letters, household accounts, recipes and personal accounts. The latter included notes on various expenses, such as postage, stationery, debts, dress and accessories, and were sometimes entered in personal pocket diaries or 'pocket books'. These were small leather-bound volumes fastened with a brass clasp.

During the course of the day a lady might take a music lesson or simply practise. If the weather co-operated, a stroll in the park, a 'walk-out' to visit nearby neighbours, or 'riding-out' in the carriage might be contemplated. The gown of the morning was changed – with the help of the ladies' maid – or a warmer outer garment simply added. The footman would have been notified to change into livery, and the coachmen readied. A footman always accompanied his mistress, protecting her among the traffic of city streets and knocking on doors for her. Away from the cities and market towns, visits to neighbours and relatives were regularly undertaken, either as day trips or more extended stays. During the season in London or Bath, the compliment of a visit from a new acquaintance would be returned.

The round of visits often included calling upon the community's poor. The Georgians' passion for society did not altogether exclude some consideration for its less fortunate members. Indeed, children of wealthy families were encouraged to make donations to charities or destitute individuals. Young Fanny Austen Knight's diaries are full of ' - - 2 [for] a poor boy' or 'gave a poor man - - 1', ' - - 2 for an old woman'). In a letter to her friend Miss Chapman, dated 1806, Fanny mentions an evening's entertainment at Godmersham Park, where the 'little ones' set up a stall in the library to sell 'toys and trinkets' to the adult company. The proceeds – at least in part – were to be given to the poor. Important ladies often had charities named after them, responsibility for which then passed on through the family. Elizabeth Austen Knight eventually took on the management of the charity that had been under the patronage of Mrs Thomas Knight.

In the early evening the master and mistress of the house, their family and guests, would dress for dinner. Following dinner, the gentlemen remained in the dining room while the ladies withdrew to their feminine domain, the drawing room, where the gentlemen later joined them for tea and refreshments. Amusements for the evening customarily included cards, music and singing, or reading and conversation, followed by a light supper and bed. A footman waited at the staircase to hand candles to the retiring guests. The ladies' maid would wait up till all hours to help her lady into her nightdress, curl her hair, see her to bed, and then fold away her evening clothes. The broader diversions of a gentlewoman included, as previously mentioned, a season in London or Bath to join in the delights of concerts, exhibitions, pleasure gardens and the theatre, shopping and select company. In addition, a sojourn in other spas, such as Tunbridge Wells or Cheltenham, and a visit to one of the coastal resorts might be undertaken. Long stays with relatives living at a distance also came into the annual social calendar.

From time to time – indeed, with extraordinary frequency – these pleasures were interrupted by childbirth. Mrs Austen had eight children, Elizabeth Austen Knight had eleven, and her sister Sophia Deedes 'was taken to bed with child' on twenty occasions. In *Northanger Abbey* ten offspring is considered a comfortable amount: 'A family of ten children will always be called a fine family, where there are heads and arms and legs enough for the number'.

## *The well-ordered nursery*

Many children, like Jane Austen herself, were sent to live with a wet nurse in the village for the first few years of life. These women were chosen for their patience and loving nature, as it was believed that mother's milk was endowed with the characteristics of its bestower. This arrangement seems to have done little harm – at least among the Austen children, who received early parental contact in the frequent visits of the Reverend and Mrs Austen. Brook John, Elizabeth Austen Knight's eleventh child, was not sent out, but rather received the ministrations of a wet nurse in his Godmersham home 'four times daily'. (Elizabeth was taken suddenly ill and died a few days after her son's birth.)

The overall care of the infant was superintended by the household's head nurse, and if the mother herself suckled the child, the head nurse was at her side. During the first month of life the child was bathed twice daily with warm water. During the second month it was advised that the water be gradually cooled to reach 'spring' temperature. After bathing, the baby received a dusting of hair powder. Contrary to the earlier custom of swaddling, infants' legs were now given as much freedom as possible. All the while the head nurse kept a vigilant eye over her charge for any symptoms of illness or infection. The diaries of Fanny Austen Knight record the usual flu, colds, mumps and whooping cough passing through the family at Godmersham Park; none of their illnesses was particularly severe. For an infected finger, Fanny received 'electrification', which, remarkably, appears to have been effective. She also mentions younger brothers and

*'Mama, don't make me beg in vain. Pray read that pretty book again!' (1808). Motherhood was perhaps the most important role available to ladies of gentle birth during the eighteenth and nineteenth centuries, for it was through the rearing of children that the landed gentry sought to perpetuate their lifestyle and values. Adam Buck's somewhat sentimental vision of the mother's role contrasts with the grimmer realities hinted at in many of Jane Austen's letters.*

*'A family of ten will always be called a fine family, where there are heads and arms and legs enough for the number'* (Northanger Abbey). *In this watercolour of the Edgeworth family (opposite) by Irish artist Adam Buck, 1787, the novelist Maria is on the far left.*

sisters recovering from inoculations for the cow pox. Their dental work – usually the extraction of teeth – was dealt with in London; Jane Austen mentions taking her nieces and nephews to see the dentist. Ill health was managed in the first instance by the housekeeper and cook, who prepared home remedies for complaints as varied as 'the Staggers', 'swell'd neck' and 'Bite of a Mad Dog'. Recipes for a range of medical treatments were given in most cookery books of the period. Thereafter, the patient was under the management of the surgeon, the physician, the apothecary or, lastly, the unlicensed practitioner. Hartfield in *Emma*, like most small towns or large villages, was typical in having only an apothecary.

Older children in the nursery were more the concern of the under-nurse, while the nursery maid saw to the housework of the rooms that comprised the nursery, keeping everything clean and neat and the fires lit. The under-nurse awakened the children at seven, bathed and dressed them, and sent them off to breakfast at the nursery table, 'in the most peaceful and orderly manner', advised *The Complete Servant* (1825). After breakfast the children were taken out for air and exercise. On returning, their hands and feet were washed, and afterwards they joined the governess in the school room for lessons. The governess, whose high office was the education and guidance of young ladies and gentlemen, was advised not to make herself too familiar with the domestic servants, and 'to conduct herself in such a manner, as never to render an apology necessary for her presence at family parties'. She taught her pupils English, literature, poetry, letter-writing, French, Italian (the language of music), arithmetic, geography, popular sciences and religion, as 'no young persons who are born to the enjoyment of fortune, and destined to fill any stations, should have these accomplishments and sources of knowledge withheld from them'. Lessons lasted until dinner in the late afternoon, which for children was always taken in the nursery. After dinner, if the weather was good, the children might again have outdoor activities; otherwise, they amused themselves with dancing, skipping-rope and dumbbells – all important for inducing exercise – or games such as chess and cards. Jane

Austen entertained her visiting nephews with bilbocatch, spillikins, paper ships, riddles, conundrums and cards. In the evening another session of instruction was undertaken, usually a combination of scholastics and art. It was the governess's further responsibility to teach needlework (both plain and ornamental), dancing, drawing, and the first lessons on the piano forte, before this task was taken over by the music master. Bed was promptly at eight o'clock.

## The training of a gentleman

Following their early years in the nursery and school room, young gentle-men were usually sent away to school. Though James and Henry Austen were taught at home by their father, the more usual practice was for a boy approaching public school age to receive a thorough grounding in Greek and Latin from a private tutor, such as the scholarly Reverend George Austen, while, if means allowed, boarding with the tutor's family. The young student would then go on to one of the public schools, such as Harrow or Eton. All six sons of Edward Austen Knight went to Winchester College, as did James Austen's son James Edward, whom Jane later teased: 'Now you may own, how miserable you were there; now, it will gradually all come out – your Crimes & your Miseries . . . how often you were on the point of hanging yourself – restrained only, as some illnatured aspersion upon poor old Winton has it, by the want of a Tree within some miles of the City.' Heroic tales of public school life abounded during the eighteenth and nineteenth centuries, but as it turned out, James Edward was happy at Winchester and 'retained all his life a warm interest in the school'. It had initially been settled that James Edward Austen was to go to Eton, and the boy and his father departed thence to make the final arrangements. But on their journey an accident with some bramble bushes tore the Reverend James Austen's clothes to such tatters that they were obliged to return home and make the trip another day. Before the second attempt was undertaken the Reverend heard something about Eton that caused him to change his mind, and he resolved to send his son

Winchester College, from the Warden's Garden, c.*1816. Most young boys of the period were sent away to school from about the age of eight. Although Jane Austen sympathized with her nephew James Edward Austen during his time at Winchester, she felt that the discipline of a public school was a necessary part of a gentleman's development.*
Opposite: *Then, as now, 'the noble game of cricket' was a favourite pastime of public schoolboys and young gentlemen. 'As the gentlemen play, the ladies look on, and altogether it is very pleasant', wrote Fanny Austen Knight to a friend.*

to Winchester. The tribulations of a young Etonian of the eighteenth century are charmingly described in a letter to his mother that cannot have failed to touch her heart:

My Dear Mama

I wright to tell you I am retched, and my chilblains is worse agen. I have not made any progress and I do not think I shall. i am very sorry to be such expense to you, but i do not think this schule is very good. One of the fellows has taken the crown of my new hat for a target, he has burrowed my watch to make wheal, with the works, but it won't act – me and him have tried to put the works back, but we think some wheels are missing as they won't fit. I hope Matilda's cold is better i am glad she is not at a schule. I think I have got the consumption the boys of the place are not gentlemen but of course you did not know that when you sent me hear, i will not try to get bad habits.

The trousers have worn out at the knee, i think the tailor must have cheated you, the buttons have come off and they are loos at the back i don't think the food is good but I should not mind if I was stronger. The peace of meet i sent you is off the beef we had on Sunday but on other days it is more stringey. There are black beetles in the kitchen and sometimes they cook them in the dinner which can't be wholesome when you are not strong. Dear Mama I hope you and Papa are well and don't mind my being uncomfortable because i don't think i shall last long . . .

Your loving but retched son

T.H.

Breaks in the school calendar heralded joyful family reunions. During holidays at home, boys liked to spend their days fishing, shooting and

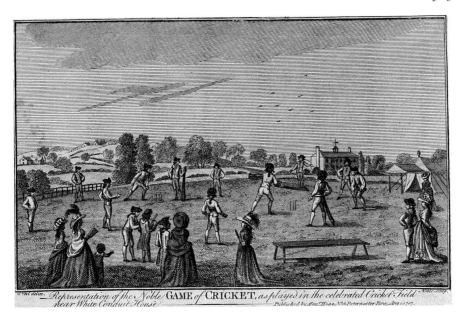

Representation of the Noble GAME of CRICKET, as played in the celebrated Cricket Field near White Conduit House. — Published by Alex.r Hogg, N.o 6 Paternoster Row, Aug 1.1787.

hunting – sports developed as part of a country squire's traditional attachment to his land and to nature. James Austen had a strong love of horses and hounds, and during his early days as a curate at Overton or Deane he kept a pack of harriers on an income that could scarcely keep a family. His son James Edward was equally keen on hunting and frequently joined in the famous Vine Hunt, with its curious breed of foxhounds. Edward Austen Knight and Edward Austen Knight the younger were both members of the Hampshire Hunt. In her pocket diary of 1809 Fanny Austen Knight wrote, 'The two eldest boys went out shooting this September for the first time & had pretty good success for young beginners. Edward killed in all 3 brace & George 1 brace besides[...]Hares, Rabbits etc. They had only 5 days partridge shooting'. In 1815 Fanny mentions another favourite pastime of public school boys and young gentlemen: cricket. 'My brothers are[...]rather mad about cricket & we are frequently having meetings[...]in the neighbourhood. As the gentlemen play, the ladies look on and altogether it is very pleasant.' Both ladies and gentlemen, young and not so young, shared an enjoyment of archery and riding. In *Mansfield Park* Fanny Price rides to maintain her health, while Mary Crawford rides to attract the attention of her instructor, Edmund Bertram. Country walks, another popular outdoor pursuit, were a particular pleasure of Jane Austen's.

A young man's education generally concluded with university, which at this time meant Oxford or Cambridge, the only English universities then in existence. Here, learning was based on the classics. It was at St John's College, Oxford, that so many Austen and Austen Knight gentlemen completed their education. Among Oxford's ancient halls and medieval traditions students could stretch their academic abilities and achieve the patina of a higher education. To be educated and knowledgeable was to be genteel, and one could almost be forgiven for being the son of a mer-

| | £. | s. | d. | DISBURSEMENTS. | £. | s. | d. |
|---|---|---|---|---|---|---|---|
| Entrance into | | | | | | | |
| Board ½    Year due as above - - - | 18 | 7 | 6 | Dentist   Hair Cutting 4/   Apothecary's Bill | | 4 | |
| Latin, Greek, and Geography - Ditto - - | 2 | 12 | 6 | New Shoes 14/   Shoes repaired 7/6-3/6 - - - | 1 | 14 | |
| Writing, Arithmetic, and English   Ditto - - | 2 | 2 | | Taylor's Bill for repairing and buttoning Clothes - - | | 8 | 6 |
| French - - - - - Ditto - - | 2 | 2 | | Coach Hire 3/6   Vacation at - - - | | 5 | 6 |
| Military Exercise - - - Ditto - | | | | Hatter's Bill 7/   Hosier's Ditto | | 7 | |
| Dancing - - - - Ditto - | | | | Mending, with Materials for Ditto - - - - | | 5 | |
| Drawing - - - - - Ditto - | | | | Gloves /.   Shoe-strings 2/   Shoes cleaning 3/6 | | 7 | |
| Single Bed - - - - - Ditto - | | | | Letters and Parcels 4/   Combs and Brush   Tooth Brush | | 4 | |
| Wine daily, by Desire - - Ditto - | | | | Hoyt's Pantheon 5/6   Speech 6 | | 6 | |
| Tea, Morning and Evening, by Desire   Ditto - | | | | French Reader 4/6 — | 4 | 6 | |
| Pure Milk, Ditto - - - Ditto - | | | | Oranges &c 3/ — | | 6 | 6 |
| Washing and Extra - - - Ditto - | 9 | | | | | | |
| Allowance Weekly - - - Ditto - | | 10 | 6 | | | | |
| Copy Books, Paper, Pens, &c. - Ditto - | | 10 | | | | | |
| Exercise Books /   Slate   Pencils   Ruler | | | | | 29 | 16 | 9 |
| Domestic Medicines /   Windsor Soap / - - | | 5 | | | | | |
| Assistants and Servants 21/   Chaplain /6 - - | 1 | 6 | 3 | | | | |
| Amount of School Charges | 29 | 16 | 9 | | 34 | 8 | 9 |

chant by possessing a satirical eloquence displayed during the university's endless debates. But it required a degree of self-motivation to achieve a genuine foundation for learned expression and to resist the allure of drink and gambling, which were also associated with the hallowed institution. John Thorpe in *Northanger Abbey*, one of Oxford's less distinguished graduates, had no perceivable interests beyond his carriages, horses and drink. In his weekly periodical *The Loiterer*, James Austen satirizes the 'Modern Oxford Man' writing in his diary:

> Eight to ten, Coffee-house, and lounged in the High-Street. ... Jack very pleasant – says the French women have thick legs. ... Went to stable and then looked in at the Coffee-house – very few drunken men. ... Went back to my room in an ill humour – found a letter from my father, no money, and a great deal of advice. ... Do think fathers are the greatest *Bores* in nature ...

The grand tour, an aristocratic tradition, had by the eighteenth century come to be considered an essential part of an upper-class education. While touring the Continent, young men were expected to gain a heightened appreciation of Roman and Renaissance cultures, evidenced by the Italian paintings and French furniture that they brought home with them. They were also expected to master foreign languages, history, politics and geography, while perfecting their diplomatic skills. However, many saw these travels as an opportunity for high living, much to the despair of Bri-

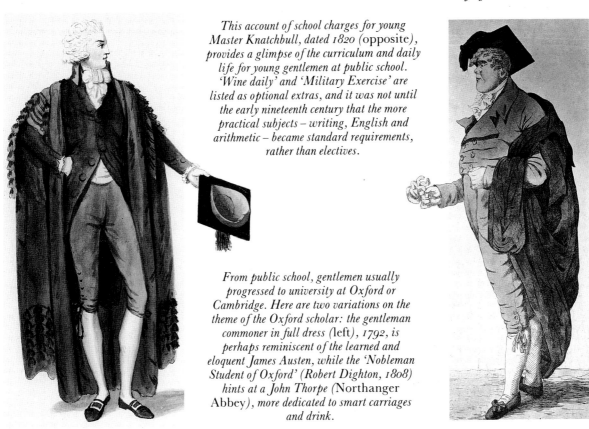

*This account of school charges for young Master Knatchbull, dated 1820 (opposite), provides a glimpse of the curriculum and daily life for young gentlemen at public school. 'Wine daily' and 'Military Exercise' are listed as optional extras, and it was not until the early nineteenth century that the more practical subjects – writing, English and arithmetic – became standard requirements, rather than electives.*

*From public school, gentlemen usually progressed to university at Oxford or Cambridge. Here are two variations on the theme of the Oxford scholar: the gentleman commoner in full dress (left), 1792, is perhaps reminiscent of the learned and eloquent James Austen, while the 'Nobleman Student of Oxford' (Robert Dighton, 1808) hints at a John Thorpe (Northanger Abbey), more dedicated to smart carriages and drink.*

tain's ambassadors. As important as cultivating a taste in art, was the cultivation of manner. Towards the end of the eighteenth century and during the nineteenth century the wealth of the nation ceased to be the reserve of aristocrats. Great fortunes were being made by the prosperous merchants of the rising middle classes, who were in turn buying vast amounts of land and, upon their newly acquired land, building great country houses like those of established aristocratic families. It became increasingly difficult to distinguish a genuine aristocrat from those who wished to mimic them, and the cultivation of knowledge and an elegant manner therefore gained greater importance as signs of true gentility.

Men born into the landed gentry, or who acquired or inherited that status, must, as their central occupation, make the best use of their assets in order to maintain their prosperity and preserve their inheritance for future generations. The continuation of this process was a fundamental need of those who cherished their land and the rights and values attached to it – a characteristic that unites men like Mr Darcy, Mr Knightley and Edward Austen Knight.

Mr Austen Knight took his responsibilities seriously. With the assistance of his land steward, his estates were improved and extended, and some lands sold in the interest of the overall holdings. Farms, cottages and other buildings were kept in good repair, rents collected, rivers and drainage managed, and timber and livestock made to produce a sensible yield, in addition to the day-to-day administration of the estate's numerous employees. Estate business necessitated regular trips throughout Kent and Hampshire, and Edward's duties as magistrate and high sheriff required frequent visits to Canterbury. In 1813 his inheritance of the Chawton estate was challenged, and a long legal battle ensued. In the end he managed to hold on to his property, though he was obliged to sell land in Kent for £15,000 and timber from Chawton for £6135 to settle the claim. But he achieved what he had set out to do – to maintain his income and keep the core estate properties intact, so that they might be passed on to his eldest son when the young man came of age.

When the eldest son of a wealthy landowner reached his majority, the event was regarded as a cause for jubilation. It marked the time for beginning the formal transfer of the estate from parent to son. When Edward Austen Knight the younger came of age, there were 'grand doings' at Godmersham Park: a ball was held for the servants and tenants, whose numbers were so great that they could not be accommodated in the part of the house that comprised the domestic offices, and beds had to be taken down from the nursery for them to dance there. The room was 'ornamented ... very prettily with branches of Laurel and lilac, & at the upper end E. K. in gold letters surrounded with boughs and lamps.' Fanny Austen Knight had the honour of opening the ball, which lasted until ten o'clock and was followed by supper in the servants' hall and lobby.

> The next day the poor people dined before the Servants Hall door & afterwards danced on the green in front of the house – we counted about 200 people and I never witnessed a more gratifying sight than the groups of dancers & smokers & lookers on etc etc. They gave several rounds of cheers & I think their [shouts] might almost have been heard at Chilham &[...]also 'God Save the King' in fine style. (10 May 1815)

The legal 'Agreement between Edward Knight elder and Edward Knight younger' involved a transfer of money, stock and properties, and arrangements for a future wife. Young Edward settled at Chawton Manor House, where he was to spend the rest of his life. Chawton Manor, up to 1989, was still in the hands of the Knight family, though it has recently been sold.

While the future for an eldest son was pre-ordained, his brothers were in the ticklish position of having to choose an occupation appropriate to their station. Very few professions or businesses were considered honourable enough for a gentleman. In *Sense and Sensibility* Edward Ferrars outlines the options for a young man of genteel birth seeking a career; Edward is himself the eldest son, but his helpless attitude is that of one born much lower in the line of succession:

> It has been, and is, and probably will always be a heavy misfortune to me, that I have had no necessary business to engage me, no profession to give me employment, or afford me anything like independence. But unfortunately my own nicety, and the nicety of my friends, have made me what I am, an idle, helpless being. We never could agree in our

*George Morland's* The Benevolent Sportsman *of 1792 portrays the Georgian landowner as he most liked to picture himself: as a generous and tolerant patron, touring his lands on horseback in order to keep in touch with his dependants, and dispensing charity to those less fortunate than himself.*

choice of profession. I always preferred the church, and still do. But that was not smart enough for my family. They recommended the army. That was a great deal too smart for me. The law was allowed to be genteel enough; many young men, who had chambers in the Temple, made a very good appearance in the first circles, and drove about town in very knowing gigs. But I had no inclination for the law, even in this less obtruse study of it, which my family approved. As for the navy it had fashion on its side, but I was too old when the subject was first started to enter it – and, at length, as there was no necessity for my having any profession at all, as I might be as dashing and expensive without a red coat on my back as with one, idleness was pronounced on the whole to be the most advantageous and honourable.

The Napoleonic war gave the army a newly elevated status, so that it became a most fashionable calling, suitable for aristocrats as well as gentlemen. Of course this applied only to officers; those serving among the lower ranks were 'the scum of the earth', as Wellington put it. Rank had to be purchased, which added to the profession's glamour; a majority cost £2600, and might be acquired through an advertisement in a newspaper, while the cost of an ensign's commission was £20,000 in present-day terms. The negotiation of a particular commission was probably more successful if accompanied by a recommendation from an esteemed friend or acquaintance. Henry Austen wrote to a Major James on behalf of 'a young friend desirous of purchasing a commission. . . . I can furnish you with every particular – age, height, name, parentage, education & fortune of the young man', said Henry, and 'you may call the young man your friend with safety'. Henry had, during his varied career, been a captain in

A Gentleman at Breakfast *(c.1775–80), attributed to Henry Walton. Although this painting considerably pre-dates the writing of* Mansfield Park, *styles of interior design were slow to change in the country, and one can easily imagine Tom or Edward Bertram enjoying a quiet breakfast and newspaper in such a room, before setting out for the morning's ride. In the portrait opposite of c.1789, Edward Austen Knight is shown on his grand tour of Europe, acquiring an appreciation of ancient art while collecting a few treasures to send home.*

the Oxford Militia. Another soldier in the militia was the roguish Wickham in *Pride and Prejudice*, who served during a time when the militia was being supplanted by the army, as it was thought a standing army was necessary against invasion; the militia was now possibly more important as a source of recruitment into the regular army. A commission in the militia was considerably less expensive than one in the army, and therefore less impressive. Captain Tilney (*Northanger Abbey*) was a captain in the army and is described as following the most fashionable calling for an eldest son. Yet even this distinguished profession had among its members those more dedicated to idle behaviour, drink and gambling, than service to the country.

Naval officers were less aristocratic than their counterparts in the army, and were drawn more from the upper middle class or gentry. It was not surprising for a country parson such as the Reverend Austen to have two sons in the navy; Lord Nelson, the hero of Trafalgar, had been a clergyman's son. Unlike the army, the navy allowed a boy who went to sea as a lowly midshipman to rise through the ranks as a result of his own efforts; but the process was accelerated if his merits were combined with influence, patronage and even purchase. In *Mansfield Park* William Price, a midshipman, despairs of becoming a lieutenant through his own abilities before he is so old as to lose all joy in the promotion. In the end, his promotion is advanced by the efforts of Henry Crawford and by a chain of influence that leads to the first Lord of the Admiralty. Advancement and the acquisition of wealth in the navy were greatly assisted during wartime, which provided opportunities for distinguished heroics and the chance to accumulate prize money, obtained by capturing enemy vessels. In *Persuasion* Captain Wentworth's rise in the world is supported by both. Though this was the glorious era of Nelson's navy, inglorious practices were rife: there were, for example, the navy's policy of protecting the slave trade, and the activity of press gangs that abducted young men and forced them into service on ships, where they suffered severe floggings, cramped contagion-ridden conditions and malnutrition. Yet in spite of these unharmonious circumstances, officers and their men achieved remarkable unity during sea battles and are perhaps best remembered for their outstanding valour.

It was more fashionable to be an army or naval officer, or even a member of the legal profession, than to be a clergyman. Nevertheless, a rector was a well-respected member of society, and in rural communities his status was second only to that held by the wealthy landowners, who welcomed him into their homes without social discomfort. The 'living' of a parish was given by the owner of an estate, so that it was not surprising for second sons to choose the church as a profession and to take up the living of the parish within their father's estate, when the position was vacated. Two of Edward Austen Knight's sons became clergymen: Charles became rector of Chawton, and William became rector of Steventon. The amount of money provided by a living varied. Many clergymen, like the Reverend James Austen, simultaneously held the livings of two or more parishes, being based at one while riding out to perform the duties of the others. This arrangement, known as plurality, would have suited Mr Collins in *Pride and Prejudice*, as he considers his task as a clergyman to involve little more than the baptizing, marrying and burying of his parishioners. On the other hand, Edmund Bertram in *Mansfield Park* feels the importance of being resident among his parishioners so as to be more aware of their needs and to provide more guidance.

James Edward Austen, like his father and grandfather before him, chose the church as his profession. He prepared for his ordination by himself at home and 'On May 29th 1824 went by Collyer's coach with W. Knight to London for ordination'. When his brother-in-law Benjamin

The Sermon, *after a painting by R. Westall, 1813. Nobles and country gentry – like the Tilneys of Northanger Abbey – attended to the rector's sermon from the comfort of the family pew.*

Lefroy took orders, the bishop only asked two questions: Was he the son of Mrs Lefroy of Ashe, and had he married a Miss Austen? When Henry Austen took orders in 1816 he went for the purpose to the bishop of Salisbury, an old friend of his father's, who put forward various questions, and then, putting his hand on a Greek Testament, said 'as for this *book*, Mr Austen, I imagine it is a good many years since either you or I have looked into it.' This conclusion disappointed Henry – who had been something of a Greek scholar – as he had looked forward to exhibiting his skills in the language. The clerical examination of James Edward Austen required him to attend two successive days at Winchester House. In the evening he attended plays, which do not appear to have affected his performance in the exams, for one year later he followed the same course and was ordained priest.

**Evening entertainment** *for ladies and gentlemen would typically include piano-playing, singing and card games. Jane wrote in 1808, 'We found ourselves tricked into a thorough party at Mrs. Maitland's, a quadrille & a Commerce table, & Music in the other room.' This piano in the drawing room at 1 Royal Crescent, Bath, made in 1798, is similar to one belonging to Beethoven.*
*Above: A table set out for cards at Stoneleigh Abbey, Warwickshire.*
*Right: Regency rosewood table with inlaid chequerboard.*

47

The Church of England, at the time of Jane Austen's writing, was in a state of flux. The aggressive doctrines of the evangelical movement that so marked the Victorian age were only beginning to touch the moral attitudes of England's population. The Georgians could be forgiving without being sanctimonious and accept minor moral infractions in conduct, providing one strove for salvation. The emphasis was on positive Christian values, rather than on expunging the sinister side of man's character. Positive values could be absorbed by reading sermons, giving attention to the service, prayers, and by attempting to duplicate good thoughts and deeds in one's life. It was not an inactive reverence. At the conclusion of 1806 Fanny Austen Knight (aged thirteen) wrote in her diary: '[the year] passes without our advancing far in the most [important] work [...] that of our salvation. May God give us grace to spend the next year in a manner more [conducive] to our eternal interest.' Two years later her diary described her daily routine, including the observance of her religion:

*Sunday morning church*
A sermon before breakfast. After breakfast go to church if possible; (if not read the psalms and lessons, say my noon prayer & read another sermon before dinner). After church, say my noon prayer, learn my [...] and epistle (or gospel, or psalm etc) say it and read my Nelson's festivals before dinner. After dinner read the psalms & Lessons, read another sermon say my Catechism and Poetry and in the evening always read *one* and sometimes *two* sermons.

Religious principles, like principles of education and conduct among ladies and gentlemen of rank and fortune, helped to shape the unique social history of the period. It was a society that encouraged self-esteem, self-improvement and, most of all, self-perpetuation through the preservation of inheritance. This was achieved through a management process that began in a well-ordered nursery and progressed through training in social rituals, transmitted from one generation to the next. A sensitivity to nature and poetry, knowledge of art, music and literature, and well-reasoned, polite discourse characterized the aristocrats and gentry, and determined how they lived. How they lived was also determined, in part, by their obsession with the display of wealth, as evidenced by the splendidly conceived and furnished houses of the age, lavish entertainments, conspicuous though elegant consumption, and zealous attention to the latest fashions in dress, as each engaged in the competition of looking his or her best.

Opposite: *Detail from an engraving of Godmersham Park, the Kent country seat of Edward Knight Esq., 1785.*

# 2·The Country House

**The bridge,** Carriage sweep and lawns to the north of Cottesbrooke Hall in Northamptonshire, a possible prototype for Mansfield Park. Built during the early eighteenth century for Sir John Langham, it was inherited during Jane Austen's lifetime by the tenth baronet, Sir James Langham, who may have been a friend of Jane's brother Henry. Inset: Two ladies taking an airing in a phaeton, from a fashion plate of 1794.

HE STATELY HOMES of England, crowning a green, picturesque landscape, illustrate to perfection the principles of balance, grace and manner. For Jane Austen, these edifices, the houses of country squires and nobility alike, were not simply the expressions of a wealthy ruling class, but represented an ideal civilization, a mixture of self-esteem, national pride and uncompromising good taste. And as such, they provided the ideal background for her novels: an orderly foundation on which to stage social folly.

Jane Austen's forebears were wealthy merchants on her father's side of the family, and solid aristocrats on her mother's, which put her on a firm footing with the leisured classes. Her father, as rector of the parish of Steventon, was welcomed – together with his family – into the households of the neighbourhood's landed gentry and well-off tenants. Furthermore, Mr Austen had the added prestige of being the representative of the community's main landowner, his cousin Thomas Knight. After 1797 Jane's brother Edward, as Knight's heir, became the local magnate, placing the Austens on visiting terms with some of the highest-ranking families in the kingdom. Thus Jane Austen was particularly well situated to study a whole range of country houses, from graceful village manors to the splendours of sprawling aristocratic estates. Her observations of real settings provided the raw materials for her writing and, through her novels, a chronicle of some of the finest examples of England's architectural past.

Several periods of domestic architecture are represented in the novels, each differing more in time than in taste. Sotherton Court (*Mansfield Park*) is Elizabethan; Mansfield Park is probably Palladian; Uppercross (*Persuasion*) is from the time of William and Mary's reign at the end of the seventeenth century; whereas Pemberley (*Pride and Prejudice*) is thought to be Jacobean, and Colonel Brandon's Delaford, described by Mrs Jennings in *Sense and Sensibility* as 'a nice old-fashioned place, full of comforts and conveniences', may be a country manor of Wren's period. But it was during the eighteenth century, into which Jane Austen was born, that domestic architecture reached its pinnacle of achievement and appreciation, in the era appropriately known as the Golden Age of the English country house.

One of Jane Austen's greatest skills as a writer – and a delight to today's social historians – is her ability to write from life, accurately depicting visual details and fragments of personalities, then combining them into what seems a plausible whole, but is in fact a mosaic. Fundamental to her technique was a highly developed awareness of her environment in all its aspects; '3 or 4 Families in a Country Village' is what she chose to 'work on', uniting them with an elegant setting and then playing out their social dramas. Her own country village of Steventon undoubtedly provided some inspiration for her delightful craft.

*Steventon Rectory in Hampshire, Jane's home between 1775 and 1801, in a sketch by her niece Anna Lefroy.*

# The Georgian landscape: through Jane Austen's eyes

Despite the rumblings of the Industrial Revolution, throughout Jane Austen's lifetime her beloved Hampshire countryside maintained its serene rural appearance. The natural beauty of gently sloping hills, wide open meadows and timbered fields was gradually being seamed with fast-growing hedgerows and the occasional low stone wall imposed by the laws of enclosure. Yet the uneven patchwork appearance of the land, as it increasingly became divided into individual holdings, had an attractive sense of order about it. Interspersed with the land at varying intervals were hamlets, villages, and the occasional market town initially visible from a distance by the church spire. Within the towns and villages were the manor houses, so placed by their ancient feudal roots, and out beyond the clusters of buildings, screened by undulating, landscaped parklands, were the country seats of baronets.

In *Mansfield Park* we receive a view of the standard village plan as Miss Bertram delivers a running commentary to her carriage companions, summarizing the assets of Sotherton Court, the ancestral manorial estate of her fiancé, Mr Rushworth:

> Here begins the village. Those cottages are really a disgrace. The church spire is reckoned remarkably handsome. I am glad the church is not so close to the Great House as often happens in old places – There is the parsonage; a tidy looking house, – those are alms-houses, built by some family. To the right is the steward's house; he is a very respectable man. Now we are coming to the lodge gates; but we have nearly a mile through the park still [before reaching Sotherton Court].

*A **wide range of country houses*** *was familiar to Jane Austen, from comfortable village manors to grandiose estates. She was a frequent visitor to Deane House, Hampshire (below), home of the John Harwoods, who were close friends of the Reverend Austen and his family. In spite of near financial ruin, the young John Harwood managed to hold on to his ancestral home, though at the cost of great personal sacrifice. Above left: Rowling House, Kent, where Jane's brother Edward and his wife Elizabeth, née Bridges, lived 1791–8, before moving to Godmersham Park (opposite) – seen here from the Ionic temple in the grounds. Goodnestone Park (above right), home of Elizabeth's father, Sir Brook Bridges, remained almost a second home to the Austen Knight family.*

The neighbourhood of Steventon, where Jane spent the first twenty-five years of her life, was fairly standard among the small villages of Hampshire. Thatched cottages nestled among clusters of trees, and an occasional manor house of mellow brick, partly viewed through hazel hedges and set at a reasonably imposing distance from the lane, blended into a scene of comfortable dignity. Steventon Church, built in the twelfth century, and a tawny Tudor manor stood apart from the village and the rectory, at a distance of three-quarters of a mile, so that the Austens were obliged to walk along a muddy cart track or through woodlands in order to attend services. Sycamores, elms, and a yew tree mentioned in the Domesday Book sheltered the small church. Inside, a boxed pew was provided for the Digweed family, tenants of the adjacent manor, who are often mentioned in Jane Austen's letters; their name, which the Austens, not surprisingly, found amusing, now populates the churchyard.

The rectory itself was somewhat grandiose, with its wide curving drive, and had been considerably rebuilt to accommodate the Reverend Austen and his growing family. It was a two-storey house with dormer attic windows and a balanced arrangement of Georgian sash windows set into a flat facade, which was given character by a trellised front porch. On one side of the rectory grew a plantation of elm, chestnut and fir, and at the back was an old-fashioned garden, formally arranged with a turf walk bordered by strawberry beds, leading to the garden's focal point: a sun dial. The garden was overlooked by the rector's bow-windowed study, which made up one of two wings extending from the back of the house. The rest of the rectory's ground-floor interior included a dining or common sitting room, a small parlour and a kitchen. Upstairs were seven bedrooms plus three attic rooms. Decorative elements were limited to whitewash; beams were exposed – even before this feature was thought to evoke rustic charm – and the joins between walls and ceilings lacked cornices. Although the interior of the house tended toward practicality, the Austens owned some good pieces of furniture, of which they were proud – this was the age of supreme craftsmanship in furniture-making.

A mile's walk from the rectory was the elegant Ashe Park, the Holders' residence, where Jane was a frequent guest for dinner and cards. In a letter to her sister Cassandra, she wrote of dining there 'tete a tete' – evidently a pleasant experience: 'To sit in idleness over a good fire in a well-proportioned room is a luxurious sensation.' Ashe Park, created during the reign of James I in the early seventeenth century, was a symmetrically arranged mansion of mellow red brick, set off from the road by a long, tree-lined drive. Beyond the gardens and woodlands surrounding Ashe Park, at a distance of approximately one mile, was Ashe House, the home of Jane's particular friend, the interesting Mrs Lefroy. Ashe House had all the pleasing symmetrical features of the early Georgian period: classical lines, evenly spaced white sash windows set in red brick, and a delicate fanlight surmounting the front door. Inside, it was compact and practical, with dividing doors between the morning and dining rooms that could be opened to allow space for dancing. On from Ashe House, in the neighbouring parish of Deane and other adjoining parishes, there were similar, though varied, arrangements of church, rectory, tenanted village cottages, farmhouses, manor houses and an occasional stately, aristocratic mansion.

Jane Austen's social category, the country gentry, lived in an assortment of attractive and respectable country houses. In the middle of the range would be a Sotherton Court, with its seemingly endless, lofty rooms, dignified ancestral portraits and ample furniture. Less grand was Steventon Rectory, with its reception rooms, study and bedrooms all rather plain and unadorned. Upwards on the scale beyond Sotherton Court was the realm of a massively opulent aristocratic pile such as Chatsworth, with its 32,000 acres.

It was land that counted for everything in English society during the eighteenth century and the early part of the nineteenth century. Wealth, status, political power and even marriage prospects were directly affected by the size of one's property. The squire of a manor was like a little monarch in his village. Some, like Sir Thomas Bertram (*Mansfield Park*), became Members of Parliament, able to call upon the political support of their tenants and neighbouring landholders. The usual purpose in becoming a Member of Parliament was to promote the rights of landowners, giving them more power; thus, they ran the country. Sir Thomas further maintained his property through income from his land in Antigua, the profits of which probably relied on the labour of slaves. Interestingly, Francis Austen denounced landowners in the West Indies for their 'harshness and desperatism'. The smaller holdings of the yeoman farmer, consisting of a couple of hundred acres or less, all but disappeared during this period as a result of taxes, the enclosure laws and the increased cost of land. The rich became richer through the acquisition of land by wealth or marriage – which in turn produced political favours which led to more wealth. From the king to the poorest in the land there was a pyramid of power and property, so that it became the ambition of every man to secure a fortune, to buy a large piece of land, and on it to build an elegant country house. Having acquired an estate, it became a prepotent ambition to hold on to it.

The acquisition of property was mainly achieved by either or both of two methods: inheritance or purchase. One could inherit land through the legal means of fee-tail or fee simple. A fee simple estate was one inherited by any heir of the owner. Fee-tail land was only inheritable by a specific class of heirs, usually the grantee's lineal male issue or – failing this – related males. Mr Collins in *Pride and Prejudice* inherits the Bennets' Longbourne home, a fee-tail estate, for lack of a Bennet son. Where there was more than one son in the same family, the fee-tail estate usually went to the first born.

Jane Austen became very familiar with the laws of inheritance through the experiences of members of her own family – for example, that of her elder brother Edward, who through his adoption by Mr and Mrs Thomas Knight, inherited the vast country estates of Godmersham Park

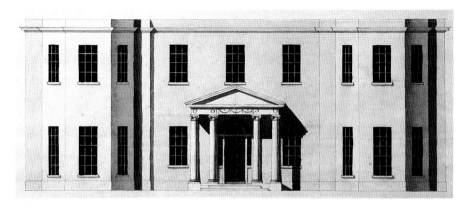

*Elevation of the original central block of Godmersham Park, built in 1732. Pavilions were added c.1780, and Edward Austen Knight carried out further alterations after Mrs Knight's death in 1812; Jane remarked in 1813 that 'the improvements within are very great'.*

in Kent and Chawton in Hampshire. In 1791 Edward married a Kent neighbour, Elizabeth Bridges, daughter of Sir Brook Bridges the Third of Goodnestone Park. On her father's death in the same year, the title and the great house were inherited by Elizabeth's brother, and her mother and unmarried sisters went to live at nearby Goodnestone Farm. The newly married couple first settled at Rowling House, a small but comfortable manor house on the Bridges' Kent country estate. The house, with its pleasing Georgian facade, now painted white, lies secluded among trees and is approached from the lane along a short, tree-lined drive. Inside, the rooms are snug, with dimensions appropriate to their Jacobean origins. From the upstairs windows one can look out over the surrounding fields and farmland that make up the open, level terrain between Rowling House and the village of Goodnestone, with its dignified church tower, at approximately one mile's distance. Jane stayed at Rowlings in 1794 and again in 1796. During the year of the second visit she began work on *Pride and Prejudice*, then called 'First Impressions', several chapters of which are set in Kent.

In 1798 Edward and Elizabeth moved to Godmersham Park, which had been vacated by the widowed Mrs Knight in favour of a smaller establishment, so that Edward could assume his awesome responsibilities as owner of two great country estates. Jane often visited her brother and his family of eleven children at Godmersham Park. Her visits generally lasted several weeks at a time, and she came to love his magnificent house and surrounding parklands. Godmersham Park is worth closer inspection, for it offers an important tie between Jane Austen and the workings of a vast estate. From this vantage point she was also able to study the social plottings, ceremonies and snobbishness of the leisured classes, which are depicted again and again in her novels.

The house, erected in 1732, is an elegant early Georgian building of red brick with stone dressings (at one point in its history the brick was painted over in a gloomy stone colour). Although it has been enlarged and altered over the years since Jane Austen's visits, the interiors of the great entrance hall and north drawing room remain as they were then, sumptuously decorated with plasterwork and woodwork of the highest quality in the Palladian – Burlington School – style. The marble composition chimneypieces are also outstanding and exquisitely treated.

The park of six hundred acres that encircled the house consisted of timbered, sloping hills and deep valleys that were once stocked with deer. The approach from the road, along a sycamore avenue, led to an attractive stone bridge over the River Stour, and thence to the entrance lodge. In the eighteenth century, in connection with the landscape planting of the park, two temples were erected on adjoining knolls overlooking the house. From the garden at the back of the house the lawn gradually inclined southwards to an Ionic temple surrounded by a plantation of trees. Eastwards, across the river, a Doric summerhouse was similarly situated. Jane Austen is said to have written parts of her novels in these temples – and it is certain that she wrote letters from Godmersham, of which the following is a part: 'Yesterday passed quite *à la* Godmersham: the gentlemen rode about Edward's farm, and returned in time to saunter along Bentigh with us; and after dinner we visited the Temple Plantation, which, to be sure, is a Chevalier Bayard of a plantation. James and Mary are much struck with the beauty of the place.' On the death of Edward Austen Knight in 1852, Godmersham passed to his son, who altered part of the interior of the house and extended the domestic offices. It had been his intention to live there, but he never did so, remaining instead at Chawton House, and Godmersham was eventually sold.

Edward Austen Knight's dual inheritance of Godmersham and Chawton encompassed considerable land holdings, as well as most of the property and tenancies within each parish, including the village church, rectory, farmhouses, cottages and so on. Chawton Great House was a large Jacobean building of stone and flintwork, with arched windows and

*Chawton Great House, the Hampshire seat of Edward Austen Knight, which until very recently continued in the possession of the Knight family. Built in the seventeenth century, it is remarkably unchanged since the years of Jane Austen's numerous visits there between 1813 and 1816.*

a somewhat cold ambience. Perhaps this is why it too was painted on the exterior, though it has subsequently, and mercifully, been restored. Surrounding the house were pleasant gardens banked by a woodland walk. In a letter of 1813, Fanny Austen Knight provided her favourite correspondent, Miss Chapman, with a colourful description of Chawton House, giving it a slightly Gothic aura, no doubt for the sake of her reader:

> This is a fine large old house built long before Queen Elizabeth I believe & there are such a number of old irregular passages etc. etc. that it is very entertaining to explore them & after when I think myself miles away from one part of the house, I find a passage or entrance close to it, & I don't know when I shall be quite mistress of all the intricate and different ways. It is very curious to trace the genealogy of the Knights and all the old families that have possessed this estate, from the pictures of which there are quantities, & some descriptions of them have been routed out, so that we are not at a loss for amusement. There are quantities of trees about the house (especially Beech) which always makes a place pretty I think.

Another interesting case of fortunate inheritance within the Austen family concerned Mrs Austen's branch of the family tree, the Leighs, and a cousin, the Reverend Thomas Leigh, rector of Adlestrop in Gloucestershire. The Reverend Leigh's cousin, Mary Leigh, died, leaving him the ancestral home and estates of Stoneleigh Abbey. As the wording of the will was ambiguous, the Reverend's lawyer advised him to take immediate possession of Stoneleigh Abbey in order to thwart any other possible claims. Mr Leigh, who had hitherto lived a comfortable, though mundane, existence, followed his lawyer's advice and immediately set out for Stoneleigh together with his cousin, Mrs Austen, and her daughter Jane, who were his guests in Gloucestershire at the time.

Stoneleigh Abbey was perhaps the most aristocratic country mansion Jane had ever visited. Mrs Austen, writing to one of her daughters-in-law, gave an excellent description of the house as they found it in 1806:

> This is an odd sort of letter. I write just as things come into my head. I will now give you some idea of the inside of this vast house, first premising that there are forty-five windows in front (which is quite straight with a flat roof) 15 in a row. You go up a considerable flight of steps (some offices are under the house) into a large Hall; on the right hand is the dining parlour, within that the Breakfast room, where we generally sit, and reason good 'tis the only room (except the Chapel) that looks towards the River. On the left hand of the hall is the best drawing room, within that a smaller; these rooms are rather gloomy Brown-wainscot and dark Crimson furniture; so we never use them but to walk thro' them to the old picture gallery. Behind the smaller drawing room is the state Bed Chamber with a high dark crimson Velvet Bed; an alarming apartment just fit for a heroine; the Old Gallery opens into it. Behind the Hall & Parlours is a passage all across the

*Stoneleigh Abbey in Warwickshire, inherited by Mrs Austen's cousin, the Reverend Thomas Leigh, in 1806.*

house containing 3 staircases and two small back parlours. There are 26 Bed Chambers in the new part of the house & a great many (some very good ones) in the old.

The mention of forty-five windows is of interest; perhaps Mrs Austen, with an eye for thrift, was quietly calculating the window tax, first levied in 1696 for defraying the expenses of the recoinage of silver during the reign of William III. Houses were assessed at two shillings a year, and tax was added according to the number of windows (on ten to nineteen windows the additional tax was four shillings, with increments upwards). The tax was often increased during the eighteenth century, though it was reduced in 1823 and repealed in 1851.

Stoneleigh Abbey consisted of an Elizabethan east wing – the original part of the house, which had been built on the site of the abbey's south transept – connected with the early eighteenth-century west wing by means of a long gallery one floor above ground level, on the site of the abbey's south aisle. The multi-windowed west wing was almost overwhelming when first seen on approaching from the long, tree-lined carriageway past the fourteenth-century gatehouse. The smooth stone exterior, with its weighty regularity, was somewhat sombre, though the mass and scale of the building – contrasting with the broad green lawns – cannot have failed to impress. The house in all its combined parts was first occupied in 1726. It had been designed and built by Francis Smith, a well-known Warwick architect, and took twelve years to complete. Externally, Smith's design remains unaltered; internally, there has been little change, though the original oak panelling survives in only two rooms. The panelling was replaced by elaborate plasterwork during the ownership of the fifth and last Lord Leigh, who came of age in 1763 and died in 1786, leaving Stoneleigh and all of his estates to his sister Mary for her life, and thereafter to the nearest male heir of his kin and name. Thus it was, that on the death of Mary Leigh in 1806, the Reverend Thomas Leigh came to Stoneleigh Abbey.

Daylesford, the ancestral home of Warren Hastings, a long-standing friend of the Austen and Leigh families, was less familiar to Jane, unlike the extraordinary history of its owner. Throughout his career in India, Hastings' ambition had been to buy back the property of his forebears, which had passed out of his impoverished family a few generations before. Shortly after his famous and costly trial, Hastings was put in funds in the form of a £50,000 interest-free loan from the East India Company. With this and his pension he was able to acquire the family plot, though he was forced to overpay substantially – a measure of the importance to him of his hereditary tie.

Hastings chose Samuel Pepys Cockerell (1753–1827) of the East India Company as his architect for Daylesford. Cockerell was later to build the Indian-inspired extravaganza Sezincote, in Gloucestershire, which attracted the Prince Regent's visit in 1807 and influenced the design of the Brighton Pavilion. The exterior of Daylesford was of the finest quality Cotswold stone, the only Indian affectation being a great mosque-style dome. Inside, however, Hastings' fondness for Indian culture was reflected in a sculptured marble chimneypiece depicting a Hindu sacrifice, and in the ivory furnishings and Indian silver. Beyond all this was a showiness of opulence, grandeur and more than a touch of fanciful decorative confectionery. Immediately beneath the dome was Mrs Hastings' boudoir, with a circular ceiling painted to resemble the sky and lit by concealed windows. London craftsmen lodged in the village for a year, adding decorative flourishes to the cornices and shutters, picked out in shades of pink and green, and varnishing mahogany sashes, as well as gilding plasterwork leaves, grain and honeysuckle. The house also boasted the latest comforts, not least of which was a Bramah water-closet, an early form of flushing toilet.

Eliza, Hastings' god-daughter, and Henry Austen were regular visitors to Daylesford, and Eliza's first visit was made in August 1797, a few months before her second marriage. From Cheltenham she wrote:

> One of my principal inducements for coming here was the neighbourhood of my old friends the Hastings's whom I am just returned from visiting. They have got a place called Daylesford, which is one of the most beautiful I ever saw. I will not wrong it by endeavouring to give a description of it, and it shall therefore suffice to say that the park and grounds are a little paradise, and that the house is fitted up with a degree of taste and magnificence seldom to be met with.

Jane Austen and her mother visited the Reverend Thomas Leigh at Adlestrop Rectory in Gloucestershire in 1806; it was from there that they suddenly departed for Stoneleigh Abbey. Daylesford was less than two miles from Adlestrop, and it appears they found time to visit their important friend and to inspect his extraordinary house. Jane commented to Cassandra on a painting she had seen there: *Mrs Hastings at the Rocks of Colgong* by William Hodges.

*The west front of Daylesford House in Gloucestershire, home of Warren Hastings, built between 1789 and 1793. It appears that Jane visited Daylesford in 1806, when she would have admired the impressive statuary chimneypiece in the drawing room (below) carved by Sir Thomas Banks.*

## An enduring national style

Throughout the eighteenth century kings, nobles and gentry alike were all busy designing and building their country houses, landscaping their estates, or improving existing properties in the prevailing fashionable taste. Across England attractive residences, from aristocratic palatial edifices to comfortable roomy manors, were being erected, while their surrounding lands were shaped into a thematic, picturesque union of house, gardens and parklands. It was an age of increasing wealth, of an expanding world market and almost rampant consumerism. A notion for what was fashionable and a sophisticated appreciation of the arts and sciences were no longer confined to the select upper classes. The English classical architectural styles, in particular, were being sought after and copied from the middle classes upwards, as the well-travelled Daniel Defoe so aptly commented:

> Every man now, be his fortune what it will, is to be doing something at his place, as the fashionable phrase is, and you hardly meet with anybody who, after the first compliments, does not inform you that he is in mortar and heaving of earth, the modest terms for building and gardening. One large room, a serpentine river, and a wood are become the absolute necessities of life, without which a gentleman of the smallest fortune thinks he makes no figure in his country.

Whereas wealth and land had previously demarcated the social boundaries, now cultural sophistication and aesthetic appreciation elevated one's social position. The increasing popularity of the grand tour was to foster an overwhelming and permanent change in British domestic architecture, resulting in an enduring tradition of a national classical style, with its variations copied and re-copied across England, Scotland and Ireland.

Where there is money, creativity is allowed to flourish. During the seventeenth and eighteenth centuries this phenomenon took the form of patronage. Richard Boyle, third Earl of Burlington, was one of the greatest patrons of the arts and sciences, and as a distinguished architectural scholar in his own right, he – more than any other individual – was responsible for the fixed tradition of national taste and for the revival of Inigo Jones' Palladianism. Palladianism was a version of Italian Renaissance architecture systematized and propagated by Andrea Palladio (1508–80), whose wealthy Venetian patrons demanded elegant classical houses on their country estates – not unlike English eighteenth-century squires. His style, based equally on a study of Roman buildings and the writings of Vitruvius, was carefully tailored to meet their requirements, and by publishing his work, together with easily understood diagrams, in the *Quattro Libri*, he produced a model that could be followed throughout Europe. In England it was first taken up by Inigo Jones (1573–1657), surveyor to James I and Charles I, whose style superseded, though it did not immediately replace, the ill-understood classicism of Elizabethan and

Jacobean houses. It was Jones' Palladianism that was revived by Lord Burlington and which became standard in Jane Austen's time – a style based on symmetry, the correct use of classical orders, and a combination of dignity with practicality.

It was during the early eighteenth century that a national style was achieved. England was looking for a patriotic architectural theme – a symbol of Whig supremacy – not influenced by the French, as the baroque designs of Christopher Wren had been. Colen Campbell, a Whig follower, published the first volume of *Vitruvius Britannicus, or The British Architect* (1715) under the patronage of the second Duke of Argyll. It was this book, extolling the virtues of Jones and Palladio, and with one hundred exquisite engravings, that sparked the interest of the Earl of Burlington, who soon departed for northern Italy in order to study Palladianism first hand. While in Italy, Burlington met and became the life patron of William Kent (1685–1748), a versatile artist who greatly distinguished himself as an architect, landscape gardener, interior decorator and furniture designer through his poetic ability to unite formal classical principles and elegant rooms with the randomness of nature. Burlington financed the second volume of *Vitruvius Britannicus* in 1717. With other publications, such as Kip and Knyff's *Noblemen's Seats* (1709), Kent's *Designs of Inigo Jones* (1727), Batty Langley's *Treasury of Designs* (1740) and James Paine's *Plans and Elevations of Noblemen's Houses* (1783), this popularized the national style and provided models for country builders as well as for professional architects. The high standards exemplified in these publications spread across a broader social scale; they were carefully reproduced by gentlemen seeking to recapture the enduring quality and precise craftsmanship of clear horizontal lines balanced by pediments and elegant porticos, epitomized in the facades of Roman temples. The reasoned application of the classical orders, with various modifications and enhancements, remained the standard throughout the eighteenth century and well into the nineteenth. Thus the influence of Burlington and the multi-talented Kent was to last throughout the Georgian period.

Neo-classical architecture, which began to appear during the second half of the eighteenth century, was dominated by the tireless Robert Adam (1728–92) and his brothers. It offered a purer interpretation of the ancient forms, in that it was based on direct observation of Greek and Roman architecture, rather than on the model received through the intermediaries Vitruvius and Palladio. Adam's style was a blend of several classical styles, but combined primarily Greek, Roman and Renaissance Italian influences, from which he created his own stamp. His work was characterized by delicate colour and the free use of ornamentation to embellish the traditional symmetries. This treatment gave Palladianism a certain gracefulness, which appeared on the exterior of a building in the form of a thinly pilastered front, scored stucco and 'Venetian' windows, and on the interior as refined plasterwork in classical motifs decorating friezes, chimneypieces and doorcases, strung together with delicate festoons. Adam also invented a composition that allowed 'stick-on' mouldings to be mass-produced and made available to builders throughout the country. The curving room, elliptical or semi-circular, with arches and curved niches, was another characteristic of Adam's style. To fit these new shapes he also designed carpets and furniture of a complementary colour and theme, bringing fluidity and harmony to the whole architectural dissertation.

A classical house required a classical vista of picturesque and decidedly English scenery. Just as Palladianism had in part been a reaction against the French influence in architecture, so had the formal geometric, Versailles-type garden plan of axial and radial avenues, parterres and canals, been dispensed with. The view was laid open and irregular, woods were moved, and streams altered or added to create a meandering, though contrived, naturalness. Farm animals and wildlife were held at bay by the installation of William Kent's invention, the 'ha-ha': a sunken barrier created by digging a trench along the perimeter of one's property, allowing the view to appear never-ending, and so called from the exclamation supposed to have been shouted as the owner or one of his guests came upon it unexpectedly. A ha-ha at Sotherton Court is mentioned in *Mansfield Park*.

Lancelot Brown (1716–83) was an avid disciple of the 'picturesque' and full of brisk helpfulness when offering an opinion on a property's possibilities. He acquired his name 'Capability' from his confident appraisals of clients' acreage – 'great capability of improvement here', being the usual conclusion. Brown rolled the countryside right up to the house, thereby capturing it in a picturesque study of stately order and rambling wooded hills, gracefully framed by a serpentine river. To further comple-

*Jane and Cassandra Austen often enjoyed the annual ball given at Hurstbourne Park by Lord Portsmouth, whose son was sent to study with the Reverend George Austen in 1773.*

*The picturesque outlines of Strawberry Hill, Twickenham, Horace Walpole's
highly influential Gothic villa.*

ment this image, classical or Gothic temples, bridges, follies and artificial
ruins were artfully scattered across the landscape. Brown, working with
the existing features of a site, improved what he found by accentuating the
undulating curves of the terrain, and by bringing into focus carefully
arranged woodlands separated by long sweeps of lawn.

While classical symmetry remained the predominant architectural
theme in Georgian England, an increasing interest in informal landscapes
and a cultivated sensitivity to irregular, picturesque concepts encouraged
principles opposed to Palladian order, resulting in a taste for fantasy and
emotionalism. The stern laws of balance and order had their reaction in
disorder. The words 'irregular' and 'romantic' aptly describe the first off-
shoot movement – the Gothic Revival.

The taste for England's Gothic past began as a literary idiom and
spread to art, architecture and decoration. Horace Walpole, the leading
intellect of this movement, was inspired to disperse Gothic zeal in the
creation of his rococo castle, Strawberry Hill, complete with battlements,
tracery and a 'cabinet' that resembled an oratory; the design of this room
was so convincing that a visiting French ambassador felt obliged to
remove his hat when entering it. In describing the attractions of Gothic
taste, Walpole wrote:

> One must have taste to be sensible of the beauties of Grecian architec-
> ture; one only wants passions to feel Gothic. . . . It is difficult for the
> noblest Grecian temple to convey half so many impressions to the
> mind as a cathedral does of the best Gothic taste . . . the priests . . .
> exhausted their knowledge of the passions in composing edifices
> whose pomp, mechanism, vaults, tombs, painted windows, gloom
> and perspective infused such sensations of romantic devotion.

Catherine Morland of *Northanger Abbey*, her heart full of Gothic romanticism, was disappointed with the improvements that she found when visiting General Tilney's Abbey: 'To an imagination which had hoped for the smallest diversions, and the heaviest stone-work, for painted glass, dirt and cobwebs, the difference was very distressing.' Horace Walpole further underscored the enthusiasm for Gothic taste in the publication of his historical novelette, *The Castle of Otranto* (1764), steeped in medieval mystery, which fostered an onslaught of Gothic romances. One of these, *The Mysteries of Udolpho* (1794) by Mrs Ann Radcliffe, was read by Catherine Morland's friend Isabella Thorpe. Some of the Gothic romances were even enjoyed at Steventon Rectory; and in the neighbouring parish of Sherborne St John, the influence of Horace Walpole found a more tangible expression in its representation at the Vyne, the grand ancestral residence of Mr and Mrs William John Chute.

Jane Austen had attended lavish balls at the Vyne, and her brothers had enjoyed the famous Vine (later Vyne) Hunt. Her eldest brother James, while vicar of Sherborne St John, had often dined there, taking along his young son James Edward, who was to become Jane Austen's first biographer. William John Chute's predecessor, John Chute, had been a firm friend of Horace Walpole, and – next to Walpole himself – was considered to be the leader of the 'Strawberry Hill' school of design. John Chute even chose to have himself painted holding an elevation in his hand for the Gothicizing of the entire exterior of the Vyne. As it happened, after much correspondence between Walpole and Chute, they settled on the Gothic style for only one room, the ante-chapel, which after so much consideration turned out to be rather vague and unsuccessful. Ironically, after this Gothic diversion, John Chute chose a style of classical purity for the house's major alteration. The architectural history of the house is also interesting; built on the site of a vineyard, it was basically Tudor, and was extensively altered in the seventeenth century by John Webb, another disciple of Inigo Jones. Webb erected a Corinthian portico against the north front, one of the earliest in England and a clear example of Palladianism, though it was constructed fifty years before Lord Burlington was born.

A more extensive example of domestic Gothic architecture within the Austen family, and one well known to Jane, was Adlestrop Park, the ancestral home of her mother. Adlestrop Park, located in the heart of the Cotswolds, had been the property of the Leighs since the Reformation; Mrs Austen's father had been born there, and it had passed to her uncle, and through his descendants to her cousin's son. The last-named, James Henry Leigh, and his wife were occupants of the Park in 1806, when Jane and her mother were guests at Adlestrop Rectory. Built by Mrs Austen's great-grandfather, William Leigh, who died in 1690, Adlestrop Park was a handsome building with formal gardens and extensive pleasure grounds. Between 1750 and 1762 the house was 'improved' in the Gothic style by architect-designer Sanderson Miller (1717–80), best known for his work on Lacock Abbey, who carried out his alterations between bouts of madness. The result, however, was a well-reasoned arrangement of del-

*Originally built in the reign of Henry VIII, the Vyne, near Basingstoke in Hampshire, has been altered over the centuries to reflect changing fashions in architecture. The ante-chapel was transformed into a rather flimsy Gothic style by John Chute, with the assistance of Horace Walpole. James Austen was a regular dinner guest at the Vyne, and his son was a member of the Vyne Hunt.*

icate bay windows capped by lacy parapets and crocketed pinnacles.

In planning a country estate, the house is usually constructed as the first stage, and the garden subsequently laid out around it. However, with the increasing taste for picturesque irregularity, the customary sequence was often reversed; the setting was beginning to dictate the architectural style, in order that it might be in keeping with the natural characteristics of the overall scene. Thus, Humphry Repton (1751–1818), who during the late Georgian and Regency periods became one of the most famous landscape gardeners in England, often worked closely with architects where the new construction of a house was being undertaken, in order to maintain the interplay between building and setting. The house, according to Repton's ideal, should 'partake of the quiet and sequestered scenery' rather than dominate it. He had a high regard for Lancelot Brown, but considered that his open expanses of lawn were too naked, especially when immediately surrounding a house. He felt that the connection between house and grounds ought to flow, as well as be habitable, and he tended toward the introduction of pleasure grounds that linked the house with the landscape without interfering with the overall scene: 'The more essential part of Landscape Gardening is apt to be overlooked in the general attention to the picturesque, which has often little affinity with the more important objects of comfort, convenience, and accommodation.' An all-encompassing Repton layout merged the house with the garden through a series of contiguous interior rooms flowing on to a conservatory, and from there to a shrubbery walk, flower garden and aviary – the whole then linked in character and position with the larger landscape. The complete design often included the construction of an entrance lodge, a small sample of the main house, which would become another accessory of the view – 'when time has thrown its ivy and creeping plants over fresh hewn rocks, the approach will be in strict character with the wildness of the scenery'. Even a rustic cottage might be built into the distance, 'to give an air of cheerfulness and inhabitancy to the scene which would without it be too sombre'.

The gardens at Adlestrop Park were laid out by Repton, and his advice was also sought on a new drive to the rectory. More extensive were his suggestions for the improvement of the landscape surrounding Stoneleigh Abbey. Perhaps Jane had these properties in mind during the writing of *Mansfield Park*, when Mr Rushworth, having visited his friend's newly landscaped Compton, contemplates improvements to his own property, Sotherton Court:

> 'I wish you could see Compton', said he. 'It is the most complete thing! I never saw a place so altered in my life. I told Smith I did not know where I was. The approach *now* is one of the finest things in the country. You see the house in the most surprising manner. I declare when I got back to Sotherton yesterday, it looked like a prison – quite a dismal old prison.'
> 'Your best friend upon such an occasion', said Miss Bertram calmly, 'would be Mr. Repton, I imagine.'
> 'That is what I was thinking of. As he has done so well by Smith, I think I had better have him at once. His terms are five guineas a day.'
> 'Well, and if they were *ten*', cried Mrs Norris, 'I am sure *you* need not regard it. The expense need not be any impediment. If I were you, I should not think of the expense. I would have everything done in the best style, and made as nice as possible. Such a place as Sotherton Court deserves everthing that taste and money can do. You have space to work upon there, and grounds that will well reward you.' ...
> 'Smith's place is the admiration of all the country; and it was a mere nothing before Repton took it in hand. I think I shall have Repton.'

In laying out the grounds of a vast country estate, not only the visual aspects, but also its productivity were taken into account. The country gentry ate well from their own produce: beef and lamb from extensive pastures, fish straight from streams and ponds, venison, game fowl and rabbits had for a day's sport, pork and chicken from the farms, an array of vegetables and fruits nurtured in kitchen gardens and hothouses, cheeses and rich cream from the dairy. Mrs Austen's ancestral home, Stoneleigh Abbey, produced an abundance not unlike the yield of most other large estates, as indicated in a letter that she wrote in 1806 to one of her daughters-in-law:

> I do not fail to spend some part of every day in the kitchen garden, where the quanity of small fruit exceeds anything you can form an idea of. This large family, with the assistance of a great many blackbirds and thrushes, cannot prevent it from rotting on the trees. The

*In his* Fragments on the Theory and Practice of Landscape Gardening, *Humphry Repton, who received so many accolades from Mr Rushworth in* Mansfield Park, *shows how he transformed the view 'From My Own Cottage in Essex'.*

gardens contain four acres and a half. The ponds supply excellent fish, the park excellent venison; there is a great quantity of rabbits, pigeons, and all sorts of poultry. There is a delightful dairy, where is made butter, good Warwickshire cheese and cream ditto. One man-servant is called the baker, and does nothing but brew and bake. The number of casks in this strong-beer cellar is beyond imagination; those in the small-beer cellar bear no proportion though, by the by, the small beer might be called ale without misnomer.

At Northanger Abbey the garden contained a number of acres 'such as Catherine could not listen to without dismay, being more than double the extent of all Mr Allen's, as well as her father's, including church-yard and orchard. The walls seemed countless in number, endless in length; a village of hot-houses seemed to arise among them, and a whole parish to be at work within the inclosure. . .'. Even Steventon Rectory was self-sustaining, with a few cattle and sheep, a small poultry yard, and a productive vegetable garden.

With the restart of the Napoleonic Wars in 1803 came the threat of invasion, which remained even after the Battle of Trafalgar in 1805 and consequently curtailed the landscape gardening business. The opportunities to arrange scenic parklands had begun to disappear, and with the end of hostilities, landscape gardeners found themselves called upon to decorate plots of only a few acres surrounding villas and cottages ornés. These two new types of house were of similar proportions – one elegant, the other countrified and often thatched. John Nash (1752–1835), whom Humphry Repton – and his son George – had worked with, invented the cottage orné, a genteel example of rusticana that allowed its owner to become completely immersed in the picturesque, though diminished setting. The village of Adlestrop contained at least one cottage orné for Jane

Austen's scrutiny. In the polite vernacular the word cottage took on a somewhat grander meaning; Mrs Elliot's 'cottage' in *Sense and Sensibility* included a dining parlour, a drawing room and a saloon. And in *Persuasion*, Uppercross Cottage, 'with its verandah, french-windows and other prettinesses [was] quite as likely to catch the traveller's eye as the more consistent and considerable aspect and premises of the Great House'.

It is the Regency period that is most closely associated with Jane Austen, for it is during this period that all of her books were published, starting with *Sense and Sensibility* in 1811 – though in fact this book (originally titled 'Elinor and Marianne') had been written in 1795. The term 'Regency' applies to social customs, fashion and the arts over a time span of some twenty years, starting at the beginning of the nineteenth century. As a constitutional form, the Regency was the period during which the future King George IV was statutorily acting for his father as head of the realm; it began with the passing of the Regency Bill in 1811, and ended with the death of the king in 1820. George III, who came to the throne in 1760, therefore reigned throughout Jane Austen's lifetime. Spiritually, Jane remained a child of the eighteenth century into which she was born, as evidenced by her surroundings, the values expressed in her writing and choice of subject matter, and even by the lifestyle of her characters, particularly within the environment of their country houses.

The Regency style of architecture was in the broadest terms either classical or Gothic. In its classical manifestation it retained the traditional proportions and dignity, though with smoother and more restricted embellishments. Externally, brickwork was often given a veneer of stucco, which was then painted white – or occasionally blue or pink, especially in coastal resorts. Gothic houses continued to be built, though as the Victorian era approached, this style lost all traces of its earlier delicacy, and assumed a sterner and more fortified arrangement of battlements, arched windows and parapets. Within Jane Austen's villages of Steventon and Chawton there does not appear to have been a notable house constructed during the Regency, though the interior decoration of most of the stately homes known to her would have displayed the prevailing fashions in furniture and decor. In the novels, apart from references to cottages, Hartfield in *Emma* is the only 'modern' Regency arrangement, with its flowing interiors and French windows.

The Regency ended with the construction of the most explosive burst of architectural fantasy, a reaction to over one hundred years of classical reason – the incredibly exotic Royal Pavilion in Brighton, built by John Nash for the Prince Regent. Not surprisingly, it had its critics. One of the Prince's guests at the Pavilion remarked: 'St Paul's came to Brighton and pupped'.

It was back in Hampshire, in the village of Chawton, that Jane Austen was to spend the last seven and a half years of her life: the most productive years of her writing career. From Chawton Cottage she was once again a participant in, and observer of the workings of village life, the social tangles among the inhabitants of cottages, manors, and the Great House it-

*'Though careless enough in most matters of eating, he [General Tilney] loved good fruit'*
*(Northanger Abbey). Many of Jane Austen's contemporaries had forcing gardens*
*constructed, like those drawn by Repton in 1816, to keep them supplied with exotic fruits.*
*The 'pinery' at Northanger Abbey 'yielded only one hundred' pineapples.*

self. Chawton Cottage, built in the seventeenth century, reputedly as an inn, had been occupied by the steward of the Knight estate until 1808. In 1809 Edward made the cottage available to his widowed mother, Mrs Austen, Jane and her sister Cassandra, and their friend Martha Lloyd. Jane was clearly pleased with her new surroundings, for she expressed her delight in an amusing little verse written to her brother Francis:

> Our Chawton home, how much we find
> Already in it, to our mind;
> And how convinced, that when complete
> It will all other Houses beat
> That ever have been made or mended,
> With rooms concise, or rooms distended.

It did not beat all other houses in scale or design, or decoration to the interior, but it was 'snug' (a Jane Austen compliment for compact but commodious) in its setting, in spite of the Winchester traffic. Prior to her arrival at Chawton, Jane described the cottage in a letter of November 1808 to Cassandra:

There are six Bedchambers at Chawton; Henry wrote to my Mother the other day, & luckily mentioned the number – which is just what we wanted to be assured of. He speaks also of Garrets for store-places, one of which she immediately planned fitting up for Edward's Manservant – and now perhaps it must be for our own – for she is quite reconciled to our keeping one.

*The Jacobean mansion* at Chawton and the surrounding estates were inherited by Edward Austen Knight, and in 1809 he provided Chawton Cottage (inset) as a home for Mrs Austen, Jane and her sister Cassandra, together with their friend Martha Lloyd. It was here that Jane spent the last seven and a half years of her life.

The entrance to the cottage was changed, and the ground-floor rooms reorganized for the sake of privacy and a more attractive approach through the garden. The small stone-floored entrance-way opened immediately onto the drawing room, with its low ceiling and central beam. Beyond this, a vestibule, with an ample bookcase, connected the drawing room with the dining parlour. The dining parlour was used for general living as well as for eating, and it was here, at a small pedestal table, that Jane Austen is thought to have written some of her best novels. Upstairs were six smallish bed-chambers. Outside, the garden provided seclusion, with a shrubbery and an orchard, and space enough for exercise along a gravel walk. Across the yard were the granary and the bakehouse, with its bread oven and copper-lined wash tub. The exterior of the house was of smooth red brick, and the whole somewhat asymmetrical, showing a history of alterations. Most of the front windows were Georgian sash painted white; casement windows of a previous era remained at the back; and set in the high-pitched roof were two dormer attic windows. As part of the rearrangement of the ground floor, Edward Austen Knight blocked up a large window that had faced onto the busy road, and cut a new window into the drawing room wall overlooking the garden, to provide a view for the ladies of the house and to give the ground floor, with its connected rooms, a cheerier aspect. In the new window, of the sash type and painted white, the top four panes had insertions of carved wood formed into arches – the Austens' gesture of Gothic whimsy.

## From fact to fiction: the houses of the novels

It is generally accepted that in her writing Jane Austen never copied directly from actual places, and that attempts to link visual details in the novels with real settings or houses would prove fruitless. An interesting exception to this view is incorporated in Sir David Waldron Smithers' *Jane Austen in Kent* (1981). In the chapter entitled 'Chevening' he makes a convincing identification of Rosings in *Pride and Prejudice* with the very real Chevening in Kent, and of Mr Collins' parsonage with that of Jane Austen's cousin the Reverend John Austen.

Chevening is located near Sevenoaks, the home of Jane's great-uncle Francis Austen, whom she visited at the Red House in 1788. During that visit Jane also visited her cousins in the neighbouring village of Seal, and (judging by Sir David's extensive research) it is highly likely that she paid her respects at Chevening as well, and went on to use it as a model for Rosings. Another link discovered by Sir David was that in 1796 Chevening belonged to the Stanhope family. The first Lord Stanhope's mother had been called Catherine and appeared in the Chevening records as 'dau. of Arnold Burghill', providing an almost ready-made name for the chatelaine of Rosings, Lady Catherine de Bourgh.

In 1940, in an article written for the *Times Literary Supplement* entitled 'The Last of Mansfield Park', Ellinor Hughes lamented the demolition of Harlestone House in Northamptonshire, which she claimed may have

*Chevening, near Sevenoaks in Kent, 1828. Was this the model for the home of the formidable Lady Catherine de Bourgh?*

been the prototype for Mansfield Park. The village plan of Harlestone and the layout of the mansion (which was called Harlestone Park in Jane Austen's day) matched the descriptions in the novel. Similarly, Mansfield Common, to which Miss Crawford was escorted by all the young party except Fanny Price, had all the attributes of Harlestone Heath. Inside Harlestone House there were folding doors between the billiard room and the study that resembled the novel's descriptions of Mansfield's billiard room, with its communicating doors to Sir Thomas' room. Furthermore, *Mansfield Park* was written between 1811 and 1814, just after Humphry Repton's alterations to the house and park. Repton's talents are much discussed in the novel, as we have already seen. In an early edition of *Mansfield Park*, published in 1820, the frontispiece shows two prints of Harlestone Park, one before and one after Repton's alterations. In the Clarendon Press edition of the novels, edited by Dr R. W. Chapman, the frontispiece is again of Harlestone Park. Ellinor Hughes goes on to claim that Jane Austen visited Harlestone Park and other houses in Northamptonshire. Unfortunately, no evidence exists to show that she was ever in that county. In fact, the evidence is to the contrary, as indicated by a letter to her sister Cassandra of 29 January 1813, in which she seeks information on the Northamptonshire countryside: 'If you could discover whether Northamptonshire is a country of Hedgerows I should be glad again.' In a subsequent letter to Martha Lloyd, of 16 February 1813, she refers to her friend's efforts to gain information on the county: 'I am obliged to you for your enquiries about Northamptonshire, but do not wish you to renew them, as I am sure of getting the intelligence I want from Henry, to whom I can apply at some convenient moment "sans peur et sans reproche".'

*'**Sunshine after Rain**':Repton sought to transform his clients' properties as dramatically as sunshine and rain transform an English garden. In his* Fragments on the Theory and Practice of Landscape Gardening *(1816) he expressed his appreciation of the picturesque beauties of nature, which he always aimed to retain or create artificially in dealing with any commission – as witnessed by his 'before and after' drawings of Harlestone Park in Northamptonshire (*above*), used to illustrate the 1820 Clarendon Press edition of* Mansfield Park.

The well-travelled Henry, Jane's brother, was a useful source of information who could be called upon to verify the accuracy of some of the visual details in the novels, i.e. Northamptonshire's hedgerows. As explained by Park Honan in his book *Jane Austen, Her Life* (1987), Henry may have provided a link between his sister and Northamptonshire through his friendship with Sir James Langham, the owner of Cottesbrooke Hall (a second house associated with *Mansfield Park*). What is certain, is that there exists a considerable amount of correspondence between Henry's banking partner James Tilson, of the firm Austen, Maunde and Tilson, and the Langham family. Mr Tilson was also known to Jane: 'Mr Tilson admired the trees', she wrote of his visit to Edward's Chawton House, 'and grieved that they should not be turned into money'. Furthermore, Henry or Mr Tilson may have learned of Harlestone and of Repton's alterations there through Sir James, who was known to Harlestone's owner Robert Andrew as his co-trustee for a neighbouring estate.

Cottesbrooke Hall, built between 1700 and 1712 during the reign of Queen Anne, is an exquisite example of early eighteenth-century architectural perfection. Its architect is reputed to have been Francis Smith, who also designed Stoneleigh Abbey. The background of the Langham family is remarkably similar to that of the Bertrams – even their names – suggesting that Jane Austen collected more than just geographical data from Henry. These relationships are further reinforced through other, though perhaps more trivial pieces of information. Mr Andrew's sister-in-law was a daughter of the Isham family of Lamport, Northamptonshire, and her mother, Mrs Isham, was the recipient of a locket through the last will and testament of the deceased Mrs Leigh of Stoneleigh Abbey; as part of the same will, Jane Austen inherited a 'centre ring'.

Harlestone House was demolished in 1939, though the magnificent classical stables survive. Cottesbrooke Hall today remains appropriately elegant, as if it were still the country seat of either a Sir James Langham or a Sir Thomas Bertram. In Warwickshire, the still splendid Stoneleigh Abbey, some forty miles distant, has also been linked with *Mansfield Park* – though not so much with the mansion by that name as with the novel's Sotherton Court. The chapel in the great house was remarkably like the chapel that exists within Stoneleigh Abbey, both in its decor and proportions:

> 'Now,' said Mrs. Rushworth, 'we are coming to the chapel, which properly we ought to enter from above, and look down upon.'
> They entered. Fanny's imagination had prepared her for something grander than a mere, spacious, oblong room, fitted up for the purpose of devotion – with nothing more striking or more solemn than the profusion of mahogany, and the crimson velvet cushions appearing over the ledge of the family gallery above.

The interior description of Sotherton also reminds one of Stoneleigh:

*The chapel at Stoneleigh Abbey, Warwickshire, with its 'profusion of mahogany', like that of Sotherton Court in* Mansfield Park.

under Mrs. Rushworth's guidance [they] were shewn through a number of rooms, all lofty, and many large, and amply furnished in the taste of fifty years back, with shining floors, solid mahogany, rich damask, marble gilding and carving, each handsome in its way. Of pictures there were abundance, and some few good, but the larger part were family portraits, no longer anything to anybody but Mrs. Rushworth.

The view from the windows on the west front at Sotherton 'looked across a lawn to the beginning of the avenue immediately beyond tall iron palisades and gates', as at Stoneleigh Abbey. Then there are all those windows at Sotherton – 'more rooms than could be supposed to be of any use than to contribute to the window tax'; on the Abbey's west wing there are forty-five.

*The greater part of Stoneleigh* – *with the exception of its medieval foundations and Elizabethan east wing – was built* c.*1714 for Lord Leigh by Francis Smith. Externally, the mansion today remains largely unaltered. The library* (opposite) *retains its original panelling. The fourteenth-century gatehouse and a side view of the house* (below).

One of the hallmarks of Jane Austen's writing – her vivid character-izations compiled of several fragments of real personalities – undoubtedly also applies to the houses in her novels. Mansfield Park is a particularly good example, in that it may very possibly have been composed of both the genuine Harlestone House and Cottesbrooke Hall. However, it is also important to keep in mind the contribution that Godmersham Park must have made, since it was better known to Jane than any other grand country estate.

It is astonishing that so many of the great houses Jane Austen knew and loved still exist today, two hundred, three hundred years and more since they were first envisaged, and for the most part they exist with their former glory intact, as proud and beautiful as ever, crowning the country's most exquisite landscapes. One wonders at the architectural achievement that produced such longevity of taste and appreciation, for even today the styles, incorporating balance, order and symmetry, continue to be copied. It is this creative inheritance that links us with the past, and allows us to imagine the lives, aspirations and pleasures of the original owners of these grand – or not so grand, but always graceful – houses.

Amid the finery of their elegant halls, one can almost hear the echo of a piano forte softly playing somewhere in the background, and, from the dining room, the polite tones of dinner guests and the occasional muffled clink of crystal touching mahogany; off in the distance, the gentle pounding of horses' hooves, as a carriage approaches the forecourt. . . . But the people are gone. It is the houses that remain, and which – like Jane Austen – have conquered time.

> It was a large, handsome, stone building, standing well on rising ground, and backed by a ridge of high woody hills; and in front, a stream of some natural importance was swelled into greater, but without any artificial appearance. Its banks were neither formal, nor falsely adorned. Elizabeth was delighted. She had never seen a place for which nature had done more, or where natural beauty had been so little counteracted by an awkward taste. They were all of them warm in their admiration; and at that moment she felt, that to be mistress of Pemberley might be something!
>
> PRIDE AND PREJUDICE

Opposite: *Detail from Robert Adam's design (c.1766) for the drawing-room ceiling at Mersham-le-Hatch in Kent, home of Fanny Austen Knight from 1820.*

# 3 · Interior Styles

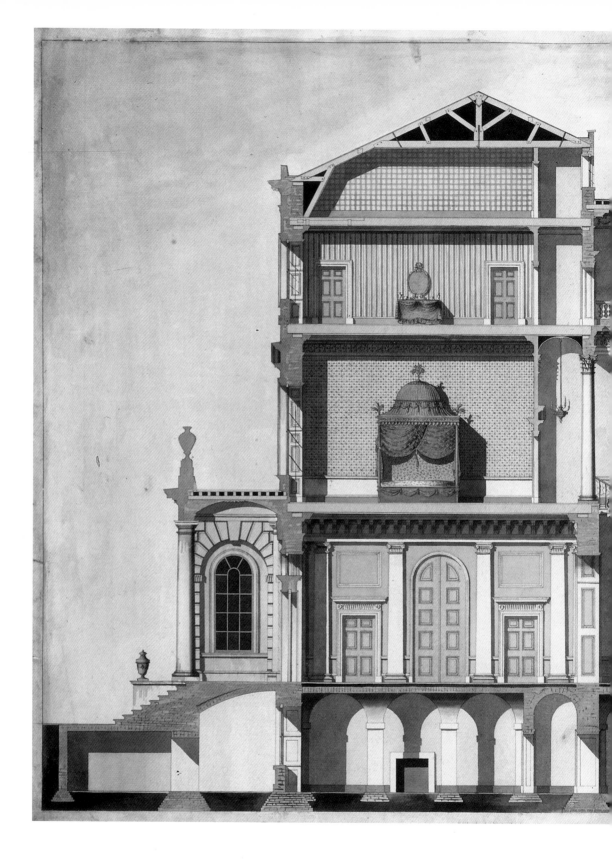

***Cross-section of a town mansion,***c.1774, *by John Yenn (1750–1821). The contrast
between the imposing, classically inspired hallway and reception rooms – complete with
marble statuary and elaborately carved cornices – and the greater variety of pattern and colour
in the rooms above is typical of the period's taste in interior design.*

HE EIGHTEENTH CENTURY and the early nineteenth century comprised an era of unparalleled creativity and beauty in furniture, pottery and interior design, no less than in architecture, landscape, art and music. The impetus for this intense artistic activity was the patronage of increasingly wealthy, knowledgeable and often similarly talented aristocrats. As the eighteenth century progressed, the spread of an informed appreciation of aesthetic achievement from the wealthy elite to the middle classes resulted in a more generalized awareness of design, particularly of domestic architecture and furnishings. This may be one reason why Jane Austen did not find it necessary to fill up her readers' senses with visual details. However, the fact that her work remains timeless is in part the gift of her genius for evoking settings, houses and the layout of rooms with the minimum of information.

In spite of high inflation caused by the wars with France, the greater social spread of wealth, coupled with an expanding world market, created a mania for consumerism. The upper classes were virtually spoilt for choice in the case of almost all goods. For the home there was a sudden increase in the range of furniture, textiles, accessories, carpets, wallpapers and so on. In order to establish the necessary credentials of wealth and position, many gentlemen, like General Tilney in *Northanger Abbey*, were seemingly in a race to update the furnishings of their country houses to meet with the newest fashionable taste.

## From order to artful chaos: in the Adam style

Before the Regency period of design (*c.* 1790–1820) comparatively little is known of what interiors actually looked like. Few significant changes were made to the interiors of country houses because of the tremendous initial investment required; materials were of the highest quality, and buildings and furnishings were made to last. Rooms not in daily use were closed up and saved for important company; furniture was covered when not in use or otherwise protected with loose covers. Susanna Whatman (1752–1814), the wife of a well-to-do Kent merchant, advised her housemaid to close the blinds in the drawing-room windows each morning to protect the furnishings from the sun. The room was to be kept dusted, including the chairs and sofas, the mahogany rubbed, and the covers shaken. In 1800 she wrote: 'I hope the sun is kept from the pictures and furniture. The blinds won't always exclude it.' Because of the cost, time and planning involved in setting up an eighteenth-century country house, the interiors must have looked simple, with a few well-made, quality pieces of furniture customarily arranged against the walls, surmounted by a sparse arrangement of pictures. This kind of simplicity was also characterized by formality and order. By contrast, the Regency heralded an age of clutter, with suites of rooms flowing one on to the next, all with the look of industry – newspapers scattered about, books opened, portfolios of prints set out to be admired – so that people gathered in the same room could be engaged in different activities and separate conversations. Paradoxically, this need to appear occupied must have been more restraining than the earlier custom of drawing chairs into a formal circle for conversing with one's guests. This latter tradition was deplored by Humphry Repton, however. In his *Fragments on the Theory of Landscape Gardening*, published in 1816, he illustrated the two arrangements and wrote a poem to accompany his pictures:

> No more the *Cedar Parlour's* formal gloom
> With dulness chills, 'tis now the *Living-Room*;
> Where guests, to whim, or taste, or fancy true,
> Scatter'd in groups, their different clans pursue.
> Here politicians eagerly relate
> The last day's news, or the last night's debate . . .
> Here, books of poetry, and books of prints,
> Furnish aspiring artists with new hints . . .
> Here, 'midst exotic plants, the curious maid,
> Of Greek and Latin seems no more afraid . . .

The transformation from order to artful chaos was begun with the Scottish-born architect Robert Adam. His predecessor William Kent had set the stage for architect-designed interiors, but Adam's 'total-look' rooms, with co-ordinated ceilings, walls, floors, chimneypieces, furniture, accessories and even door handles, were the height of extravagance at a time when exhibiting extravagance was coming into fashion, marking a significant social change. Adam is credited with bringing the neo-classical style to England. This taste for the architectural designs of ancient Greece, Rome, and even Egypt, was widespread in Paris during the 1750s – particularly the Greek influence. The French had held the lead in interior decoration since the early seventeenth century; now, after the middle of the eighteenth century, England came to the fore, influencing many countries as the century progressed. While still employing the classical forms of previous generations, the change was towards a freer interpretation of these forms. Heavy ornamentation was replaced by delicate motifs in low relief. Adam preferred pastel shades on ceilings as well as walls, set off with white decoration and some gilding; indeed, Adam considered the ceiling to be one of the most important features in the interior design of a room. For more opulent interiors, such as Syon House to the west of London, he reproduced the most lavish epoch of the Roman Empire, with vivid colours, solid gilding, marble columns and statuary. For the drawing room at Syon, Adam had the walls hung with crimson Spitalfields silk, which complemented the gilded ceiling medallions of diamond and octagon shapes designed by Cipriani. The carpet, with large octagon patterns of crimson, gold, blue and brown, was designed by Adam and executed by Thomas Moore, the well-known carpet-maker of Moorfields, London.

***Robert Adam*** *considered the ceiling to be one of the most important features in the design of a room. The delicate intricacy and soft colours of this plasterwork ceiling in the saloon at Saltram, Devon,* (opposite) *are typical of his work. The painted roundels, by Antonio Zucchi, represent scenes from classical mythology. Adam was one of the first to design co-ordinated pier glasses and tables, like this example* (above) *from the dining room at Saltram, originally equipped as a library, 1768–70.*

The less grandiose Mersham-le-Hatch in Kent, built between 1762 and 1772, was the first country house that Robert Adam designed entirely from the foundations up. This house was well known to the Austen family, as it was the home of Sir Edward Knatchbull, a relation of Edward Austen Knight through his adoptive parents, and the future abode of Fanny Austen Knight, who became Lady Knatchbull in 1820. In a letter to Sir Wyndham Knatchbull, who commissioned the house, Adam referred to his intention that the architectural design be 'kept entirely plain; and as nearly adapted to what I imagine you meant, as I possibly could'. The result was a central block of six principal rooms, and two connecting wings for offices. The entrance was approached by a dignified arrangement of steps, guarded by exquisite railings and lamp standards in wrought iron. The furniture was produced by the renowned Thomas Chippendale the elder (1718–79) to Adam's specifications. Besides furniture, the firm of Chippendale, Haig & Co. provided wall hangings and all the upholstery for the downstairs rooms and bedrooms. A letter from the company to Sir Edward Knatchbull in 1778 provides details of an Axminster carpet:

> You have likewise a design for an Axminster Carpet to Correspond with your Ceiling to go into the Bow and at equal distances from the plinth all round the Room, the Expense of it will be according to their best Price about £100 – They will have a painting to make of it at large and the Colours to dye on purpose, but if you Chuse to have it made square, like your other Carpet it will be proportionably less in price and if you or Lady Knatchbull chuses any alterations in any of the Colours, by describing it properly it may be done.

The account books of Mersham-le-Hatch for the years 1763 to 1779 show that the total expenditure for building and furnishing the house was £20,526. This sum was sub-divided under the following headings:

Opposite: *This section of one side of the hall at Syon House, 1778, reveals the impact of classical example on Robert Adam's designs: carved statues and relief medallions are interspersed with orderly pilasters, coffering and festooned plasterwork garlands.*
Right: *Adam's design for the drawing-room chimneypiece at Mersham-le-Hatch, c.1766, home of Fanny Austen Knight's husband, Sir Edward Knatchbull.*

| | | |
|---|---|---|
| Building | ... | £ 16,525 |
| Chippendale | ... | £ 1,902 |
| Other furniture, carpets, silks, bedding and china | ... | £ 595 |
| Robert Adam | ... | £ 949 |
| Silversmith | ... | £ 360 |
| Portrait by Dance | ... | £ 195 |
| | | £ 20,526 |

It is not surprising that Knatchbull's building and decorating costs included a portrait. Adam felt that painting and sculpture were 'the necessary accompaniments of the great style of architecture', and for each of his houses he brought in or suggested specific craftsmen, amounting to an army of masons, painters, sculptors and cabinet-makers, as well as bricklayers, carpenters and plasterers. Paintings were chosen to suit the decor as one would choose wallpaper.

It has been said that Rosings Park in Kent, home of the formidable Lady Catherine de Bourgh (*Pride and Prejudice*), was created from the designs of Robert Adam. Described in the novel as a 'handsome modern building well situated on rising ground', it has an interior of 'fine proportion and finished ornaments'. The clue to its architect is the mention of a vastly expensive chimneypiece in one of the drawing rooms, which had cost £800. For such an important work Adam would probably have called in Thomas Carter, a mason who often collaborated with Adam and who was accustomed to executing the elaborate chimneypieces, incorporating statuary, that formed part of the background furnishings in Adam's overall schemes. Adam's designs for furniture were more delicate than the richly carved classical styles of the first half of the century. His influence was seen in carved mahogany, but also in painted and gilded beech, and in the use of harewood and satinwood veneers. With Robert Adam, the emphasis was on design, as opposed to the intrinsic value or quality of the materials; his painted furniture is a good example of this.

To appreciate an article purely for the elegance of its design was a concept that had begun to appeal to the fine senses of the upper classes, and one that could be demonstrated by remodelling and refurnishing their homes in the new style. Sir Brook Bridges (1733–91) had his Kent country seat, Goodnestone Park, completely remodelled by Scottish architect Robert Mylne (1733–1811), who was famous for his beautiful interiors at Inverary Castle. The house was enlarged by the addition of a third storey, with pediments over the five central bays of the principal facades replacing the original dormers, and the exterior was apparently rendered in stucco, though it has since been returned to brick. Inside, Mylne was responsible for three ground-floor rooms on the east front, including an oval entrance hall decorated with graceful painted walls. The rooms flanking this were given curved walls at either end. Jane Austen's letters record her stays at Goodnestone Park, the family home of her sister-in-law Elizabeth Austen (Knight), and the painted decoration in the entrance hall remains today just as she would have seen it.

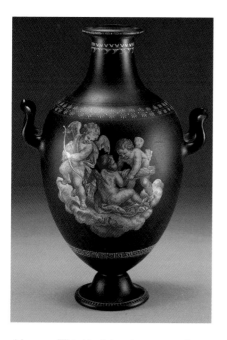

Above: *This black basaltware urn from Saltram, Devon, is typical of the work produced by Josiah Wedgwood and displayed in many eighteenth-century country houses.* Right: *One of Adam's hallmarks was the pedestal cupboard crowned by an urn, like the example shown here from Saltram, c.1780.*

The new style for a lighter, freer expression was also appearing in other areas. In dress, for example, lighter materials that swathed the contours of the body more naturally were replacing the heavily constructed clothes of the first half of the century; similarly, porcelain manufacturers produced designs of a pure, neo-classical simplicity. Matthew Boulton, metalware manufacturer and friend of Josiah Wedgwood, supplied Adam with ormolu decoration for doors and chimneypieces; he also manufactured some very fine pieces of blue john stone mounted in ormolu. For more modest interiors, Wedgwood sold black basaltware tablets, cameos and medallions copied exactly from Roman and Greek originals for 'inlaying in the panels of rooms ... or as pictures in dressing rooms'. Neo-classical furniture was varied, but displayed the kind of motifs depicted in Adam's ceilings, stucco and painted works. The Adam tradition was lent even greater delicacy in the designs of George Hepplewhite (d. 1786), in which tapering square legs replaced the curved cabriole leg. The shield-back chair design associated with Hepplewhite was a variation on Adam's

*An elegant Grecian couch by Thomas Sheraton, 1802, and chairs designed by George Hepplewhite, from* The Cabinet-Maker's and Upholsterer's Guide, *1789.*

round- and oval-backed chairs. The trend towards a delicate furniture style reached its peak in the designs of Thomas Sheraton (1751–1806). Sheraton combined compactness with portability in items such as bookcases and tables, which could be used for writing, reading, needlework or games.

Mahogany was the favoured medium for furniture craftsmen during most of the eighteenth century. Imported from the West Indies, Jamaica and British-owned islands in the Caribbean, it became increasingly popular after 1722 with the lifting of heavy import duties on timbers from the British colonies. By 1750 it had replaced walnut as the choice wood for fashionable furniture. It was extremely adaptable to changes in design, came in greater widths and, unlike walnut, was resistant to worm. For lighter items of furniture, satinwood and rosewood were more popular, and satinwood veneering, inlay and paint were used adroitly by Sheraton and Hepplewhite, as they had been by Adam. Mahogany remained a favourite for larger pieces, however.

New items of furniture of the late eighteenth century include the Pembroke table and the sideboard. The Pembroke table had side flaps which opened to create a rectangular, serpentine, or oval top with a drawer in one side, the whole supported by slender, tapering legs. 'The Pembroke', wrote Jane Austen in 1800, 'has got its destination by the sideboard, & my mother has great delight in keeping her money & papers locked up.' The sideboard of the late eighteenth century was an extension of the side table of the previous century, set against a wall and used especially in the dining room to hold silver or plate. Robert Adam created the sideboard table to fit between matching pedestal cupboards, each of which displayed an urn. One of the cupboards was generally used as a plate-warmer, and the other as a cellaret, for storing wines. The urns on top were metal-lined and usually contained iced water for drinking in one, and hot water for washing the silver cutlery between courses in the other. The top of the table was sometimes fitted with a gallery for supporting plates and knife boxes, which were made in pairs and fitted to hold table silver. In the 1780s George Hepplewhite and others merged Adam's set into a single piece of furniture to create a sideboard with a central drawer flanked by cupboards.

The dining rooms of this period were also furnished with a large central table of mahogany. Of an increasingly ponderous size, it added to the dining room's aura of masculinity engendered by the after-dinner custom of gentlemen remaining seated – smoking, drinking, discussing politics – while ladies withdrew to their sanctum, the drawing room. Early in the eighteenth century it was customary for a smaller dining table or group of tables to be used, depending on the size of the company, and at the turn of the century large tables were still being made to dismantle into two smaller tables as required.

For a formal dinner party the dining table and sideboard would boast a display of pottery from the excellent Staffordshire factories. Bone ash added to soft paste resulted in that exclusively English development: bone china. English glassware was also particularly fine. When war broke out with France in 1793, however, higher taxes were imposed which nearly crippled the glass industry. Wine glasses became smaller and thinner, so only the stems could be cut. Even Jane Austen found them diminutive: 'The Glass is all safely arrived... & gives great satisfaction. The wine glasses are much smaller than I expected, but I suppose it is the proper size' (Steventon to Godmersham, 1800). Among the sparkling tableware set out on the dining table would have been the gleam of silver or Sheffield plate, or perhaps even some items of Britannia metal. Silver was for the wealthiest households. Middle-class and profession families were more likely to have Sheffield plate, made from fusing silver to copper.

By the end of the eighteenth century the ornamentation of walls and ceilings had become flatter, with only shallow chair rails and light relief applied to friezes, cornices etc. Chimneypieces became understated compared with earlier in the century. With the increased use of coal, the aperture for the fire narrowed, and a hob-grate was fitted (a hob on each side and a grate between), made with especially designed plates of cast iron. Sir Benjamin Thomson (Count Rumford) invented an efficient fireplace with angled cheeks and a choked throat to the flue. In *Northanger Abbey* the fireplace where Catherine Morland 'had expected the ample width and ponderous carving of former times, was contracted to a Rumford, with slabs of plain though handsome marble and ornaments over it of the prettiest English china'.

*A moulded, feather-edged creamware platter by Wedgwood, c.1780, transfer-printed with a scene of classical ruins.*

*The dinner table* set for an elegant repast, with soup tureen, ashets and cover dishes all symmetrically arranged. A formal dinner consisted of two main courses, plus a dessert course, of twelve to twenty-five covers each. The dinner service is Wedgwood's 'Absalom's Pillar' design of 1812, and the knives and forks, with their green-stained ivory handles, are very similar to those owned by the Austens. The knife-blades have broad, rounded ends, so that one could eat directly from the knife as well as from the fork. Fingers were used for eating far more than is customary today, making finger bowls essential between courses. Inset: *Pistol-handled knives, forks and rat-tailed spoons, Georgian-style, in a mahogany cutlery box, together with a salver and plain hot-water jug of Sheffield plate, c.1790.* Above left: *The Georgian era produced particularly fine glassware, with mass production allowing relatively inexpensive items to grace even modest dining tables.* Above right: *A sideboard graced by a silver tea urn.*

*Worcester tea and coffee service, c.1770. The Worcester Royal Porcelain Company is the only factory existing continuously from the earliest years of English porcelain-making to the present day.*

Walls continued to be divided into dado, infill and frieze, further subdivisions being created with mouldings in light relief, paint and wallpapers. Paint colours tended towards pale and pastel shades, though rich colours such as turquoise and tangerine could also be seen. Wallpaper was becoming less expensive and, therefore, more readily used; it was available in a broad selection of patterns, as well as in the form of murals, borders, simulated marbling, stone and stucco-work. Interiors decorated with painted motifs in delicate designs made way for the look of marbling and graining.

While walls and ceilings were becoming more chaste, the arrangement of furniture was becoming more relaxed, with sofas and chairs drawn closer to the warmth of the fire, and various tables scattered about for convenience and utility. This was the period when ease and comfort began to replace order. In *Persuasion*, the daughter at Uppercross created 'the proper air of confusion with a grand piano forte and a harp, flower-stands and little tables placed in every direction'. In a letter of 1800 Jane Austen described the arrival at Steventon Rectory of two smaller tables that served the current fashion for communal activity:

> The Tables are come, & give general contentment. I had not expected that they would so perfectly suit the fancy of us all three, or that we should so well agree in the disposition of them; but nothing except their own surface can have been smoother; – The two ends put together form our constant Table for everything, & the centre peice stands exceedingly well under the glass; holds a great deal most commodiously, without looking awkwardly. – They are both covered with green baize & send their best Love.

The drawing room was arranged with sofas and chairs, sofa table, tea table, card tables, small work tables, and a piano forte. The sofa table, with falling end flaps, evolved from the Pembroke table and was intended for use at a sofa, for writing, needlework and so on. The library, with its fitted bookcases, became a room for entertaining and activity, where the fruits of the grand tour were on display. Grand houses had large library tables with leather-lined tops useful for laying out large folio books, as well as for writing and, sometimes, storage. Smaller writing tables were intended for use in the library as well as in other public rooms. In 1801 Fanny Burney, in a letter to her father, remarked:

> no room looks really comfortable, or even quite furnished, without two tables – one to keep to the wall and take upon itself the dignity of a little tidyness, the other to stand here, there and everywhere and hold letters and *make the agreeable* . . . a sort of table for a little work and a few books, en gala – without which, a room always looks forlorn.

Gillows workshops in Lancaster produced elegant writing tables made of rosewood, and a small, slim ladies' writing table fitted with compartments. In a letter to Cassandra written in 1807, Jane mentions a young

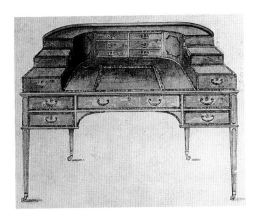

Above: *A desk designed for the Prince Regent at Carlton House.* Right: *A draped window curtain revealing a suitably picturesque view, from George Smith's* Collection of Designs for Household Furniture, *1808.*

visitor: 'she is now talking away at my side & examining the treasures of my Writing-desk drawer'.

Carpets were now being woven in strips on looms, instead of being hand-knotted, and were thus cheaper to make. Cut-pile 'Wilton' carpeting, costing between four and six shillings per yard, could be fitted or given a decorative border. 'Brussels' carpeting – the name referred to the mode of weaving – was also popular; the uncut pile consisted of loops. The second half of the eighteenth century had already introduced several notable English carpet manufacturers: Passavant at Exeter, Whitty at Axminster and Moore at Moorfields. On the Continent, Aubusson, an ancient centre of tapestry-weaving in France, produced floral-pattern carpets woven in one piece by a tapestry process, with patterns in an eighteenth-century style. The majority of these carpets appeared in England in the nineteenth century. Savonnerie carpets – made by the French national carpet manufactory established in 1726 at Chaillot – and oriental carpets continued to be seen in wealthy households, though even in prosperous houses it was not uncommon to see that very inexpensive floor covering, the floor-cloth, made of hard-wearing canvas and often painted in geometric designs to imitate stone or marble.

***The look of industry** that was becoming fashionable as an interior style is well illustrated by* The Winter Room *by Sir Charles d'Oyley, 1824. The lady is playing a harp, though the music on the piano suggests that the instrument is not long idle; the gentleman is writing, while the girl – distracted by the artist – has been reading a book. Books are stacked and scattered across the table. Seating is comfortably arranged, and even the sofa has been drawn up to the table for convenience. A fitted carpet lends the room added cosiness.*

Above left: *The carved, gilded arm of a Grecian chaise-longue covered in red velvet, from Stoneleigh Abbey.*
*Chinese hand-painted wallpapers were often exquisitely detailed, like this design from Erddig, near Wrexham in North Wales (left).*

*Furniture-makers often produced pattern books to assist their noble patrons in selecting the latest furniture styles. The delicately painted chair shown here, with its variations illustrated alongside, is similar to one owned by the Austens at Chawton Cottage.*

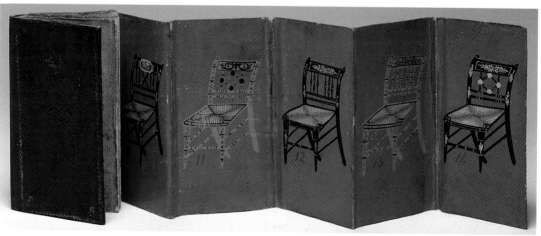

*Wedgwood remains popularly known even today for his jasperware, with white relief ornaments set against a blue, green, lavender, black or yellow background. This jug was designed by Flaxman. The black basaltware oil lamp is also typical of work produced at the Staffordshire factory.*

Window panes were becoming larger, and the English had adopted the double-doored 'French window' by the end of the century. The main reception rooms and living rooms had now come down to the ground floor from the first floor up, and the flow of rooms and activity was extended by the use of French doors that opened on to balconies, conservatories or garden walks. Larger windows added to the feeling of lightness, bringing the outdoors in. To reduce the ravages of the sun on carpets and upholstery, venetian blinds continued to be used, as well as roller blinds decorated with variously painted designs. For a time, during the 1770s, curtains that pulled up had become popular, but by 1800 divided curtains had regained their old supremacy. The 'French rod', invented towards the end of the eighteenth century, had two pulleys at one end and one at the other; cords operated from one side, drawing divided curtains back and forth along the rod. Pelmets masked rods and rings, and took the form of festoons, with bows or rosettes at tie points and trailing tails which could be either long or short. Pelmets were also used alone to decorate the top of a window, and contrasting lightweight material was sometimes used for the divided curtains below the festooned pelmet. When there were two or more windows on the same wall, window draperies were sometimes arranged to appear continuous.

From the middle of the eighteenth century chair seats were fashioned with firm, squared edges, which became characteristic of the English upholstered chair; even bolsters became squared. Chair covers were matched with the other textiles in a room, and wallpaper could be specially made to match chair seats or the overall theme of the room. Once seat furniture was moved away from the walls, the backs of these pieces began to receive more decoration. Mirror-glass placed above the fireplace was still customarily seen, and new techniques in glass manufacture allowed mirrors to be produced in larger sheets. In 1811 Jane wrote to Cassandra from the Sloane Street home of Henry and Eliza Austen that 'a glass for the Mantlepiece was lent, by the Man who is making their own.' A typical mirror design of this period was the circular, convex shape. Tall pier glasses – mirrors designed to fill the pier, or space between windows – continued to be used in tandem with pier tables. Adam had been among the first to design pier glasses and pier tables.

Pictures were displayed in a balanced arrangement from just above the dado, or chair rail – if there was one – to the ceiling. (During the early years of the nineteenth century the dado was dispensed with in some decorative schemes, allowing for a continuous expanse of wall.) Expensive oil paintings could now be copied and mass-produced in a variety of ways, such as by engraving and etching, and prints showing classical gods and goddesses, pastoral and battle scenes became popular, displayed in black or gilt frames and hung in pairs. Family portraits in heavy gilt frames continued to be exhibited with pride, together with moody scenes of European antiquity, brought to England as souvenirs of a grand tour. Paintings on tin were also fairly common; in a letter of 1801 Jane wrote to Cassandra of the dispersal of the rectory's furniture prior to the Austens' move to Bath:

> As to our Pictures, the Battle peice, Mr. Nibbs, Sir W^m East, & all the old heterogenous miscellany, manuscript, Scriptoral peices dispersed over the House are to be given to James. – Your own Drawings will not cease to be your own – & the two paintings on Tin will be at your disposal. – My Mother says that the French agricultural Prints in the best bed-room were given by Edward to his two Sisters.

Other accessories – urns, candelabra, statuary, porcelain figures and so on – adopted neo-classical motifs. Chelsea, the most outstanding English factory in the production of porcelain figures, continued to find favour. The design themes of Continental manufacturers Meissen and Sèvres were adapted by Derby, Wedgwood and Worcester, whose landscape views decorating classical shapes particularly appealed to the English public. Wedgwood's jasperware and black basaltware, based on vases of Roman and Etruscan (actually Greek) antiquity, were popularly displayed with prominence on many late Georgian tables and mantelpieces.

During the late eighteenth century lamps that burned smoky whale oil, known as peg lamps, came into existence, as did the glass-globed Argand, which burned colza seed oil. By 1800 the Argand lamp could be seen in many well-to-do households, but throughout the Georgian period most lighting was still provided by various sorts of candle, expensive beeswax candles being the most desirable.

*A needlework bed-hanging* made
during the last quarter of the eighteenth
century. Canopy, curtains and counterpane
were usually designed to match and to
complement the wallpaper and paintwork
of the bed-chamber. Right: *The Queen's
Bedroom at Stoneleigh Abbey. The
Chippendale chair and other furniture
were specially painted white and gold for
the visit of Queen Victoria in 1858.*

*A Duchess bed, designed by
Thomas Sheraton. A rather grand item of
furniture for ladies disposed to receive
visitors while reclining in the comfort and
privacy of their own bed-chamber.*

Bedrooms, also known as chambers, often contained cast-off furniture from newly appointed ground-floor reception rooms. In 1800 Jane Austen remarked that 'The little Table' had lost its position next to the sideboard – being replaced by a Pembroke – and had 'conveniently taken itself off into the best bed-room'. This spirit for fashionable renewal was demonstrated at Scarlets, formerly the Berkshire country seat of Jane Austen's aunt and uncle, the Leigh-Perrots. It had been inherited in 1836 by Jane's nephew James Edward Austen Leigh (son of her elder brother James Austen), and was described by his daughter Mary Augusta Austen Leigh:

> Meanwhile those left at Scarlets worked hard in overlooking all its contents, an occupation in which collectors of the present day would probably have been most happy to assist them, for it must have been like opening a long-closed museum. The mahogany furniture, which went back to the days of Chippendale or Sheraton, being but slightly esteemed, was placed in the bedrooms, and the drawing room was before long renovated in the early Victorian style with a flowery carpet, gilt consoles, and pale green damask curtains, though our mother was too much of an artist not to assort her colours well, so far as the tints of the day would permit, and the older furniture has outlived its period of neglect and reappeared with a shining face, to take its place as an honoured guest in polite circles downstairs. There were also a very large number of old framed prints on the walls, and the worth of these was always acknowledged, although they were taken out of their heavy frames, and, for a time, laid by. The Leigh-Perrots must in their early married life have been great lovers of china. They had collected a large quantity of blue-and-white, and a good deal of Worcester and Chelsea china, the latter being of the best date. The finest pair of vases, or figures, was at once presented to the Welbys; but a great deal remained to ornament the drawing-room.

In *Northanger Abbey* it appears that the bedrooms, though pleasant and commodious, and relatively up-to-date, received furniture of a less fashionable style than the modern profusion of furniture in the drawing rooms, dining room and other reception rooms. Catherine Morland's apartment was 'by no means unreasonably large, and contained neither tapestry nor velvet. – The walls were papered, the floor was carpeted; the windows were neither less perfect, nor more dim than those of the drawing-room below; the furniture, though not of the latest fashion, was handsome and comfortable, and the air of the room altogether far from uncheerful'.

By the middle of the eighteenth century, beds – which had earlier required steps for getting into them – were now lower. The canopy, or tester, was supported by a bedhead at the back and by columns – fluted and carved – at the front. More of the wooden framework was exposed, and thus bed-hangings became less voluminous. The tester sometimes had a frieze and cornice recalling the classical orders, or received a delicate painted decoration. Bedclothes consisted of sheets, pillows, bolsters, and a large feather quilt on a springless base, concealed beneath a decorative needlework, chintz or damask cover matched to the bed-hangings. The tent bed, so called from its resemblance to a gabled tent when its curtains or hangings were drawn, was effective in keeping out the cold, but this type of bed rarely came in sizes large enough to accommodate two people. Grandiose bed-chambers sometimes had the addition of a day bed, which during this period took the form of a single-ended couch, or chaise-longue. Sheraton illustrated a lightweight moveable piece of furniture called a 'sofabed'. Sometimes the day bed remained stationary, next to the wall or in an alcove with domed draperies, in a boudoir or dressing room, where ladies received company while reclining. Other furniture made for the bed-chamber included a toilet table with recesses for toilet articles, drawers, pot cupboard and bidet cabinet; a dressing table and mirror; a washstand on a tripod foot with a porcelain bowl above small drawers and a special soap box; a bedside commode with a drawer below and lifting-fronted cupboard drawer above; a tallboy fitted with drawers, or wardrobe, which, as designed by Hepplewhite, was a combination of cabinets separated by drawers; and a chest of drawers. The walls of bedrooms were hung with silk or paper to the dado, and a large mirror and various prints were generally arranged around the room. Wooden floors were covered with either a carpet runner or fitted carpeting. In contemplating the family's move to Bath and the equipping of their new abode, Jane wrote in 1801:

> My father & mother wisely aware of the difficulty of finding in all Bath such a bed as their own, have resolved on taking it with them; – All the beds indeed that we shall want are to be removed. . . . I do not think it will be worth while to remove any of our chests of Drawers – We shall be able to get some of a much more commo[dious] form, made of deal, & painted to look very neat; & I flatter myself that for little comforts of all kinds, our apartment will be one of the most complete things of the sort all over Bath – Bristol included.

The quest for the picturesque, which found its architectural expression in the open, flowing arrangement of ground-floor rooms and the freer, lighter form of the classical mode epitomized in the designs of Robert Adam, also led to still greater licence in architecture and interiors, and a taste for Chinese and Gothic designs ranging from the discreet to the flamboyant. Thomas Chippendale the elder produced some of his finest furniture in the Chinese taste. The elaborate 'Empire' style of interior decoration, the French term for the Imperial phase of Napoleon's career which lasted from 1804 to 1815, became popular on the Continent, in America and England. This style, inspired by Napoleon's Egyptian campaigns, attempted to copy what was known of ancient furniture and motifs – particularly Egyptian. It has been suggested that the furnishings of Henry and Eliza Austen's Sloane Street home were in the Empire style.

**The library** at Cassiobury Park, Hertfordshire, a late seventeenth-century room redecorated
in the Regency style by James Wyatt c.1800, emphasizes a sense of comfort, with chairs and
sofa drawn up to the fire and a carpet spread across the great expanse of floor.

Inset: *A mahogany secretaire in the study at 1 Royal Crescent, Bath – very much a gentleman's domain, also used as a smoking room. Displayed on the desk are a table globe, a quill pen and a Sheffield plate wax jack for melting sealing wax.*

*A Regency interior containing elements of Egyptian and antique classical inspiration, from Thomas Hope's popular pattern book,* Household Furniture and Interior Design, *published in 1809.*

Such exotic innovations were not to everybody's taste, however. The newer styles and the vast selection of furnishings available were frowned on by connoisseur, architect, author and furniture designer Thomas Hope (1769–1831). He felt that the English taste in furniture design had deteriorated, and set about designing the interior decoration of his London houses and country house in Surrey in an antique classical style that included Egyptian elements, as a model for others to follow; and indeed, his creations provided considerable inspiration for other Regency designers. The fact that it was felt design needed to be reformed, to be put back into some sort of order, perhaps indicates that the pace of change and the bombardment of variety was getting out of hand. The solidity of the old hierarchical world was quickly vanishing, as were its values. In *Mansfield Park*, the rich, vacuous Mr Rushworth considers his Elizabethan Sotherton Court to be a 'prison' that 'wants improvement . . . beyond anything'; he consults the amoral Henry Crawford for his opinion of the changes necessary to bring the landscape of his ancestral mansion into the modern taste. Another example in the novels of modernization and unbridled change brought about by wealth without deference to good taste occurs in *Pride and Prejudice*, when Jane Austen compares Rosings Park with Pemberley: the housekeeper conducts Pemberley's visitors through its lofty, handsome rooms, suitably furnished 'to the fortune of their proprietor; . . . neither gaudy nor uselessly fine; with less of splendour, and more real elegance, than the furniture of Rosings.'

# *Inside Mansfield Park*

It is tantalizing to imagine which real country houses acted as the prototypes for those in the novels. It has been suggested, for example, that Chatsworth in Derbyshire was the model for Pemberley, though this is unlikely. More convincing is the recent research linking Chevening in Kent to Rosings Park (*see* Chapter II, p.76). For the most part, however, the probability is that Jane Austen's houses, like her characters, are composites, with their parts drawn from several dwellings known to their creator. *Mansfield Park* is a particularly tempting subject for analysis in the real world, for this novel more than any of the others is restricted in its location to Mansfield Park and its environs. The house symbolizes an edifice of values, solid and orderly, in a world undergoing rapid and ungoverned change. As mentioned in the previous chapter, Cottesbrooke Hall and Harlestone House, both in Northamptonshire, and Godmersham Park in Kent may have been the originals, or at least have provided the inspiration for Mansfield Park. As it appears that Jane Austen never visited Northamptonshire, and that her information regarding that county was received second-hand through her brother Henry, it is likely that, in spite of her highly creative and vivid imagination, Henry's data regarding Harlestone and Cottesbrooke were filled out with her own knowledge of other large country houses in order to create a convincing Mansfield. Her most intimate knowledge of a vast country house was of her brother Edward's Godmersham Park, and in trying to imagine how the interior of Mansfield Park might have appeared to Fanny Price, it is probably safest to look inside all three candidates – Cottesbrooke Hall, Harlestone House and Godmersham Park.

Jane Austen enjoyed several long stays at 'dear Godmersham'. She loved the house and the lifestyle it engendered. Sadly, not many of its rooms can today be identified with those referred to in her letters; the breakfast parlour, the library 'where we live, except at meals, and have a fire every evening', the Yellow Room, in which 'I am writing at this moment', and the Chintz Room that 'I admire very much', are no longer recognizable. But the hall – where 'Fanny and Lizzie met us with a great deal of pleasant joy' – is little altered. It is 36 feet long, 24 feet wide, with its height of 20 feet enhanced by roundels above the main windows. The floor is in stone squares set diagonally with insettings of black marble, while the elaborate and profuse plasterwork is in the early Georgian style. The hall contains a domed alcove with an elaborate Grecian capital, opposite a large fireplace and overmantel with a frieze and ornaments of sculptured Carrara marble. The majestic Corinthian doorway opposite the entrance doorway, and of a similar style, led during Jane Austen's time to the staircase, which has now been moved. The other doorways have an ornateness typical of the early Georgian period, and complement the richly designed frieze and ceiling. It has been said that some of the interior embellishments are the work of Robert Adam or his brothers.

***The lavish carving*** *and directly borrowed classical motifs in the overmantel of an
elaborate marble chimneypiece at Godmersham Park contrast with the delicate rococo
ornamentation in the stairway of Cottesbrooke Hall* (opposite).

All of the principal rooms are fitted with massive mahogany doors. To the left of the hall was the north drawing room, measuring 26 feet by 22 feet, and elaborately decorated. It was remarkable for its early Georgian mirrors; the fireplace in this room was also exquisite, worked in blue and white marble and surmounted by an overmantel in the form of a portrait framed in the style of the mirrors. To the right of the hall was the dining room (22 feet by 20 feet), in which the principal features were a black marble fireplace with a large open grate, and a fine oak floor. The south rooms are plain in contrast to the lavish decoration of the hall and north drawing room, and have been considerably altered since Jane Austen's visits to Godmersham Park, but would have included the library and breakfast parlour. A plan of Godmersham Park executed in 1853 shows a second drawing room, off which were planned a billiard room and large library. Above were various principal bedrooms, dressing rooms and secondary bedrooms. The wings contained domestic offices, servants' rooms, school room and nursery suite. Today one can still appreciate the style, spaciousness and privacy of Godmersham Park, as Jane Austen found it, 'alone in the library mistress of all I survey'.

The location of Cottesbrooke Hall in relation to Northampton is near enough to match the description of Mansfield Park. Built between 1700 and 1712, it consists of a central block with forecourt and balancing wings connected by curving walls, which screen corridors. The interior shows the work of different stylistic periods. Heavy moulded wainscoting, which may have lined most of the principal rooms, survives now only in what was the entrance hall. The ceiling of the entrance hall is in the rococo style of about 1750, which is found on the ceilings of two other rooms and the ceiling of the staircase hall. The staircase is a principal feature of the house, with its wrought-iron balustrade lit by a tall, round-headed window gracing the landing. Here the elaborate stucco (actually papier mâché) decoration of the walls is of the French style known as rocaille, which achieved some popularity in England about the middle of the eighteenth century. In the larger panels an eagle and a lion rampant are modelled in relief above a design of scrolls, with the other panels framing vases of flowers. In the 1770s the west front was extended and altered by the architect Robert Mitchell. Two bow-shaped projections were added in order to provide three connected rooms, which now comprise the drawing room, the music room and the saloon. The additions and their decoration were made in the manner of Robert Adam. Today, the decoration of the drawing room is of a recent rococo imitation, while the music room and saloon are in the Adam style of the 1770s. The music room was originally painted a pale green, with a fireplace inlaid with green marble. In the saloon the fireplace has free-standing columns of jasper and a plaque with a relief of shepherd boys. Here the walls have been painted beige and the frieze coloured green, red and gold.

Between the music room and the dining room, which lies to the left of the entrance hall, runs a narrow corridor, given a vaulted treatment of semi-circular arches. A glazed door with a fanlight opens into the staircase hall. Other rooms on the ground floor could at one time have made up the library, billiard room and morning room. It has also been suggested that one of the ground-floor rooms had at some point during its history been used as a school room. Upstairs were various principal bedrooms, dressing rooms and secondary bedrooms. Below the ground floor were the kitchen, offices and some of the servants' quarters.

Among the household accounts for Cottesbrooke Hall for the years 1800 to 1811 are payments for a harp and a Broadwood piano forte – two instruments one would expect to see in any well-to-do country house of the period, though in this instance one cannot help but recall Mary Crawford's efforts in transporting her harp to the parsonage at Mansfield, where 'she played with the greatest obligingness', and the occasion when she again obliged in joining the Miss Bertrams in a glee that supplied one evening's amusement in the drawing room at Mansfield Park: 'she tripped off to the instrument, leaving Edmund looking after her in an ecstasy of admiration of all her many virtues'.

There are only slender threads of evidence connecting the Austens with Harlestone House (*see* Chapter II, p.76), but, as in the case of Cottesbrooke, the location of the mansion in relation to Northampton, and the layout of the village of Harlestone are sufficiently similar to be compatible with the novel. The estate of Harlestone belonged to the family of Andrew from the time of Henry VII. Robert Andrew was the owner of the estate and Harlestone House – or Harlestone Park, as it was then called – during Jane Austen's writing of *Mansfield Park*. Andrew vastly improved his property with the help of Humphry Repton and his sons, whose talents are much discussed in the novel. The east and west fronts of the house were modernized, and spacious detached offices erected. A sales catalogue of 1829 describes Harlestone Park as 'a very eligible and substantially built residence, erected on a unique elevation, adapted for the accommodation of a nobleman, or family of distinction'. Though Harlestone Park no longer exists – it was razed to the ground at the beginning of the Second World War – one can clearly visualize it from the description given in the sales catalogue, together with the watercolour drawings of the house and park by Humphry Repton that were used as the frontispiece of the 1820 edition of *Mansfield Park*.

The entrance to the estate was through a pair of iron gates, past rustic lodges and along an extensive carriage drive. The mansion was approached over a stone-built bridge, which led to a carriage sweep to the forecourt. The building was entered through folding glazed doors which opened on to a spacious hall paved with stone. In the hall was a fireplace that was probably in the contemporary, understated style, as the catalogue description is non-specific and only mentions it in passing. The walls were stuccoed and ornamented with pilasters. Doric columns led to an inner hall, which was lighted by a glazed dome. Adjacent to the inner hall was an ante-room, or breakfast parlour, a room frequently used for informal meetings in the novel. This room was stuccoed and painted, had a handsome cornice and a finely carved statuary marble chimneypiece.

*The kitchen* (right) *would have been dominated by a large pine work-table set out with the cook's essential equipment. In the background is an open range, complete with drip pan, cauldron and kettle, while on another wall one would expect to see a comprehensive* batterie de cuisine *(above). These copper pots, pans and moulds would have been kept well tinned to prevent poisoning by 'verdigris'. The plate-warmer (below) was usually placed in front of the fireplace in the dining room. Keeping plates – and, indeed, food – warm was a vexing problem for cooks of the period.*

Also off the inner hall was the dining parlour, which, like that at Cottes-brooke Hall, had a bowed end. The walls were stuccoed and painted to re-semble compartments, and there was an arched recess for the sideboard. The room also had a statuary marble chimneypiece, an attractive cornice, and a discreet concealed entrance for the servants.

The 'Noble Drawing Room', as it was described in the sales catalogue – the setting of much heart-fluttering in the novel – had walls stuccoed and painted, and topped by a fine cornice. The chimneypiece, again of carved statuary marble, was particularly beautiful and was enriched with columns supporting the shelf. Folding doors led to the ante-room, and there was a recess at the end which opened on to 'a capital conservatory', filled with vines and flowering shrubs, and heated by flues. If Jane Austen had Harlestone in mind as part of the mosaic that made up Mansfield Park, she neglected to mention the conservatory. It may have been added after the novel was completed in 1813, though the arrangement of draw-ing room and conservatory is typical of Repton, and Repton's major remodelling of the house was supposedly completed by about 1810.

The rooms described above were to the south, with windows 'to the ground' opening on to a paved terraced walk and lawn, and commanding a beautiful view of the park and water. The drawing room communicated with another hall, which led to the billiard room, also intended for a library. This room had a dove marble chimneypiece, stuccoed walls and 'neat Cornice'. Though this drawing room, billiard room/library arrange-ment is not an exact replica of that depicted in the novel, it bears a remark-able resemblance to Sir Thomas' room, which was located near the drawing room and had a communicating door to the billiard room. Sir Thomas had placed a large bookcase in front of the door between the rooms to give his library some privacy, making it his personal sanctuary. While he was away on business in Antigua, the young Bertrams, in their zeal to create a stage for their presentation of *Lovers' Vows*, removed the bookcase to reconnect the two rooms, so that Sir Thomas' library became the players' green room, leading on to the stage constructed in the billiard room. Soon after Sir Thomas' unexpected return to Mansfield, he came upon these alterations to his house with great surprise. From his own favourite room, with the bookcase now removed, he was able to walk through the door to the billiard room, and there found himself standing for the first time in his life upon a stage. He gave a look of offence 'towards the ceiling and stucco of the room', and 'inquired with mild gravity after the fate of the billiard table'.

On the east side of the mansion was a bed-chamber, according to the brochure, which communicated with the dining room. The walls were stuccoed in compartments and ornamented. The cornice was 'neat', and the chimneypiece made of veined marble. Adjoining and communicating were a 'Bath Room for hot and cold bathing, with a water closet, and a door opening to a corridor, supported by pillars entwined with ivy and creeper, communicating with the pleasure ground and leading to the offices'. These offices were connected by a passage and consisted of the butler's pantry, servants' hall, store closet, 'a capital lofty kitchen fitted up with dresser, shelves, sink and water laid on', a cool larder, meat and game larders, charcoal house and 'an excellent cool dairy'. Near the dairy were the scullery, wood sheds, dust hole, bake-house, with its oven and dresser, and the yards. In the basement was a large arched and paved cellar for wine, beer and ale.

From the inner hall an impressive circular stone staircase with iron balustrade, bronzed and gilt with mahogany handrail, led to the spacious landing and passage of the next floor. On this floor were a large bed-chamber with a cornice, carved and moulded marble chimneypiece, and walls papered and bordered, adjoining a dressing room with a dove marble chimneypiece and moulded architraves to the doors and shutters. There were two other principal bed-chambers with corresponding dressing rooms on this floor, including one of particular elegance that had been papered in panels with pilasters and bordered with a distinctive cornice, with its ceiling painted to resemble sky and clouds; doors and shutters were also handsomely painted and ornamented. On the same floor were four secondary bedrooms, all attractively decorated, papered, and each with a marble fireplace. These rooms were closed off from the east wing of the house, which contained the nursery, nursery sleeping room, store room and a water closet. *Mansfield Park*'s heroine Fanny Price had an 'East room', the former school room, where she kept her books, wrote letters and sought seclusion, and it was in 'the little white attic near the old nurseries' that she slept. The topmost storey of Harlestone Park had three bed-chambers on the south front, 'three Bed Rooms on the North Front and menservants' rooms'.

Outside in the stable yard were four coach-houses designed to contain twelve carriages. The parklands surrounding the mansion, including fine, thriving plantations and a pheasantry, abounded with game – a feature again in keeping with the novel and with Tom Bertram's remarks to his father about the previous autumn's shoot:

The first day I went over Mansfield Wood, and Edmund took the copses beyond Easton, and we brought home six brace between us, and might each have killed six times as many; but we respect your pheasants, sir, I assure you, as much as you could desire. I do not think you will find your woods by any means worse stocked than they were. I never saw Mansfield Wood so full of pheasants in my life as this year.

While some of the Harlestone rooms appear to correspond with the novel, the mansion and parklands seem to have been too much improved by the Reptons to be comfortable for the staid Sir Thomas and are too modern compared to the orderly, ponderous, but solid style of values that the mansion Mansfield Park represents. This again leads one to conclude that in writing the novel Jane Austen combined several houses of which she had either personal or second-hand knowledge, in order to create a particular scene or setting.

*The imposing central hall of Stoneleigh Abbey, Warwickshire: marble Corinthian pillars, heavily carved cornices, doorcases and mantelpieces, fine furniture and a stately family portrait combine to create an overwhelming impression of opulence. Every detail of the great country houses of the period was designed to achieve elegance, from the delicate fanlights (above, Stoneleigh Abbey) to the intricate papier-mâché scrolls (below, Cottesbrooke Hall).*

*The eighteenth century was an era of supreme craftsmanship in furniture-making, as these fine designs for complex pieces of inlaid furniture show.* Above: *Design for a dressing-table or commode top, 1787.* Opposite: *A commode by Robert Adam designed for the Countess of Derby's dressing room at Osterley Park.*

Of the specific interior details, furniture and layout of the rooms at Harlestone Park, unfortunately no information exists among the archives relating to the estate. Therefore, one must attempt to imagine these details – a task made far easier by the current regeneration of a vast selection of Georgian and Regency designs copied from both private and museum collections. In considering the features of Godmersham Park, Cottesbrooke Hall and Harlestone Park, one can begin to visualize appropriate colours, wallpaper, carpets and furniture by thumbing through current pattern and interior design books that reproduce period details and settings. In planning the furnishings and layout of rooms, it is best to gain some knowledge of patterns, textiles, colours and furniture by visiting some of the era's country houses and town houses that are now open to the public. There is no need to be so accurate as to produce a museum in your home, but the general features of a Mansfield-style setting can be incorporated into the overall look to pull a room together, leaving the more specific details and embellishments to personal taste.

The Mansfield interior, as I visualize it, would probably have had fairly ornate doorcases, and rich stucco and plasterwork on the principal walls and ceilings, in a style similar to Godmersham Park. The walls, if segmented with mouldings or other ornamentation, would have been painted, perhaps in one of Adam's more gentle pastel shades. Alternatively, one could imagine the space between dado and cornice hung with silk damask of a brilliant crimson, green or yellow. Both of these wall treatments pre-date the writing of the novel, but the Northamptonshire countryside, and Mansfield Park in particular, lagged behind changing fashions; the initial cost of producing such wall treatments would not have seen them easily updated. For window treatments, one has a great variety

to choose from. Festoons drawn up above the glazed area of the window – a style that was popular at various times during the eighteenth century – would not appear out of place, though heavier, divided curtains with festooned pelmets would perhaps be more likely. The pattern and colour of the fabrics used for curtains and other upholstery should of course be complementary. The furniture at Mansfield Park, which Mary Crawford wanted to replace with a more fashionable style, was probably a collection of dearly loved Chippendale or even Kentish pieces, and if we borrow another clue from the novel, used in reference to the furniture at Sotherton Court, we can expect that the furniture was predominantly made of mahogany. The best upholstered furniture, especially chairs, was usually stuffed with horsehair and covered with silk damasks or cut velvets for the drawing room, or leather, which was popularly used in the dining room and library. The best chairs would have been protected with loose covers of striped or checked linen; one feels that the frugal Mrs Norris would have been after the housekeeper and her charges to see that the furniture was re-covered once important visitors such as Mr Rushworth had departed.

On the walls, one would expect to see a touch of gilt, as on the frames of portraits, mirrors, pier glasses and sconces, or girandoles. The floors of Mansfield Park would again most likely resemble those at Godmersham Park, with stone-flagged paving or marble in the entrance hall, and floorboards polished with beeswax or scoured with damp sand in the other rooms. Although fitted carpets were becoming more generally seen in England at the beginning of the nineteenth century, it is difficult to link this style with old-fashioned Mansfield. Therefore, oriental carpets, European carpets and those with a Brussels weave seem more appropriate, with even – for Mrs Norris' sake – a few economical floor-cloths in geometric designs.

*The restrained elegance* of Georgian England lives on in this twentieth-century Manhattan apartment, which displays the timeless appeal of the era's classic designs. The half-moon table against the far wall originally came from Godmersham Park in Kent.

For the bedrooms of a Mansfield interior one would hope to indulge a freer expression of taste, with the use of colourful striped or floral wallpaper, chintz curtains and bed-hangings, and a somewhat eclectic variety of eighteenth- and early nineteenth-century furniture, all in complete contrast to Fanny Price's little white attic room.

Accessories are more a matter of personal taste, but should be grouped in an orderly arrangement. Collections of leather-bound books and portfolios of prints, as well as framed print collections and special personal possessions should be displayed and enjoyed in any setting. Family heirlooms, early plate, china figures, and table settings of the eighteenth and nineteenth centuries – of Worcester, Wedgwood and Chelsea manufacture – should receive pride of place in a Mansfield home.

The Georgian period, including the Regency, was probably the finest era of British design. The rightness of the proportions and forms, and the later simplicity of style make Georgian furnishings as easy to live with today as when they were first created. It is a great tribute to the era and, indeed, to the lifestyle of its individuals, such as Jane Austen and the characters in her novels, that these designs are so treasured even today.

*Ornamental figures, such as this porcelain fisherman produced by Chelsea c.1755–7, would have been displayed on mantelpieces in the best drawing rooms of the era.*

Opposite: *Ladies purchasing fabrics from the linendraper's Harding and Howell on Pall Mall, London, 1800 (detail).*

# 4·Fashion – and its Genteel Competitors

FASHIONABLE PROMENADE DRESSES OF 1

ANNUALLY

*La Belle Assemblée*

OR

LADY'S FASHIONABLE

*Companion.*

FOR 1814.

LONDON
Printed for Peacocks, & Bampton,
Salisbury Square.

**Young gentlewomen** *absorbed hints on the latest fashions from pocket books such as* La Belle Assemblée. *In this 1814 copy (inset), which belonged to Fanny Austen Knight, two elegant ladies promenade with their stylish shawls, bonnets and parasols. English calico printers of the late eighteenth century produced block-printed cottons that dominated the markets of Europe and North America.*

HE CONCEPT OF FASHION came into existence during the eighteenth century, and as the century progressed an awareness of stylistic trends in dress became increasingly important among the leisured classes and those who wished to imitate them. Jane Austen was an enthusiastic follower of fashion, as revealed in her letters to her sister; there are numerous references to styles, trimmings, accessories and shopping sprees. She became preoccupied with the preparation of her dress for important events and with obtaining approval: 'My black cap was openly admired by Mrs. Lefroy, and secretly I imagine by everybody else in the room' (Steventon to Godmersham, 1798); 'I wore at the Ball your favourite gown, a bit of muslin of the same round my head, border'd with Mrs. Cooper's band – & one little Comb' (Steventon to Godmersham, 1800). She was also careful to observe etiquette in dress: 'This 6 weeks mourning [for the Queen's brother] makes so great a difference that I shall not go to Miss Hare, till you can come & help chuse yourself; unless you particularly wish the contrary. – It may be hardly worth while perhaps to have Gowns so expensively made up; we may buy a cap or a *veil* instead' (Henrietta Street to Chawton, 1814).

By contrast, the novels contain only scant details of the heroes' and heroines' clothes – 'dress is at all times a frivolous distinction, and excessive solicitude about it often destroys its own aim' (*Northanger Abbey*). She disapproved of vanity and of the commonness displayed by excessive interest in the quality of other people's garments, preferring the correctness of Emma and Mr Knightley, who had 'no taste for finery or parade' (*Emma*). But, as always, her greatest admiration was reserved for elegance.

## *The changing face of elegance: 1770–1820*

At the time of Jane Austen's birth in 1775, the style of ladies' gowns was becoming more relaxed. The exaggerated, side-fullness of the mid-century was giving way to skirts extending out at the back into a shallow train that could be draped or looped by the use of cords. Hoops diminished and were finally abandoned except for Court dress. The bodice was tightly fitting, and sleeves were narrow, ending in flounces or a ruffle at the elbow. Ankles were revealed, and so stockings became more decorative, as did high, slender-heeled shoes sporting smart buckles. The 1770s was the decade when hair reached fantastic heights, extended with pads and artificial hair stretched over wire frames. Caricaturists portrayed Court ladies wearing ships in full sail, horse-drawn coaches and windmills upon their heads. To accommodate these vast hair-dos, hats for day wear increased in size and were decorated with ribbons and frills.

*The rather formal, structured fashions of the early eighteenth century are shown in this scene from* The Clandestine Marriage *by Zoffany, 1766. Jane Austen saw the play in London in 1814.*

Towards the end of the 1770s and during the 1780s 'Frenched hair', powdered and frizzed, standing out from the head and falling over the shoulders, became very fashionable, and French styles in hair and dress for both sexes were ardently followed until the French Revolution. In Fanny Burney's novel *Evelina* (1778) the heroine describes her towering, powdered head:

> I have just had my hair dressed. You can't think how oddly my head feels, full of powder and black pins, and a great cushion on the top of it. I believe you would hardly know me, for my face looks quite different to what it did before my hair was dressed. When I shall be able to make use of a comb for myself I cannot tell, for my hair is so much entangled, frizled they call it, that I fear it will be very difficult.

Fashion plates, which were beginning to appear at this time, show ladies with an exaggerated, pigeon-breasted appearance, their powdered and frizzed hair topped by enormous brimmed hats and mob-caps. The look was achieved with long corsets that thrust the bosom up and forward like a pouter pigeon – an effect further emphasized by a large, puffed-out neckerchief – while a bustle gave the pelvis the appearance of tilting back. Striped fabrics were popular, as were very bright colours, though white was always a favourite.

***Specialist journals*** *like* Le Beau Monde *spread news of recent styles for both gentlemen and ladies.*

Left: *Morning and evening dress for May 1807*. Right: *Kensington Gardens dress for June 1808*.

*Ladies in morning dress, from Heideloff's* Gallery of Fashion *for October 1807. Muslin, a fabric which became increasingly popular for its versatility, is used in both of these gowns, as well as in the bonnet worn by the figure on the right.*

The 1770s and 1780s also saw extravagant styles in menswear. In the 1770s a group of young men interested in bold fashion formed the Maca-roni Club, so called because it was thought the most extreme styles came from Italy. With their high-heeled, diamond- or pearl-buckled shoes, high powdered wigs, horizontally striped waistcoats and lace ruffles, contrast-ing with a plain coat, these elegants became the forerunners of a style in men's clothing that was to last for several decades. The country cousin of the plain coat was the frock, really a hunting or riding coat; simple and loose, it was double- or single-breasted with a turn-down collar. The dou-ble-breasted version of the frock was modified so that the top buttons were left undone to allow the lapels to fall back, and the front was cut horizon-tally at the waist to allow for more freedom of movement. During the 1780s the frock was given further refinement with the addition of a high collar, large buttons, narrow skirts and elongated tails, which made it popular for town wear. It was during this period that waistcoats became waist-length, to match the cut of the frock coat; they were double- or sin-gle-breasted and could have a small standing collar. The look of countri-fied elegance was completed with buckskin breeches fastening below the knee, and boots. As with women, the extraordinary high hairstyles began to collapse into loose curls about the face. Some gentlemen continued to wear wigs until the 1790s, though the style was now more natural, as in the tye wig, which had a single row of curls above the ears and a smooth or frizzed crown. Wigs or hair were lightly powdered until 1775, when a heavy tax was imposed upon hair powder, and the practice passed away with the century. However, during the late eighteenth and early nine-teenth centuries, liveried servants continued to apply liberal amounts of powder to their wigs as a sign of their employer's wealth and status.

The late 1780s and early 1790s saw the appearance, for women, of the 'round gown', a high-waisted garment originally designed to be loose-fitting, concealing the figure. In 1801 Jane Austen described a round gown which had been made for her at Bath:

> Mrs. Mussell has got my gown, and I will endeavour to explain what her intentions are. It is to be a round gown, with a jacket and a frock front, like Cath. Bigg's, to open at the side. The jacket is all in one with the body, and comes as far as the pocket-holes – about half a quarter of a yard deep, I suppose, all the way round, cut off straight at the cor-ners with a broad hem. No fulness appears either in the body or the flap; the back is quite plain in this form $\overline{\underline{v}}$, and the sides equally so. The front is sloped round to the bosom and drawn in, and there is to be a frill of the same to put on occasionally when all one's handkerchiefs are dirty – which frill *must* fall back. She is to put two breadths and a-half in the tail, and no gores – gores not being so much worn as they were. There is nothing new in the sleeves: they are to be plain, with a fulness of the same falling down and gathered up underneath, just like some of Martha's, or perhaps a little longer. Low in the back behind, and a belt of the same. I can think of nothing more, though I am afraid of not being particular enough.

Towards the end of the century the prevailing taste for classical sim-plicity was reflected in fashion. The high-waisted dresses became seem-ingly devoid of stays and were now seen to cling to the body in natural folds. Some women emphasized this look, and their forms, by wearing dampened gowns over buckskin undergarments, mimicking the appea-rance of ancient Greek statues. Men also adopted the slim silhouette, with tightly fitting buckskin breeches descending below the calf to meet 'Wel-lington' or 'Hessian' boots. Pantaloons soon replaced breeches and were topped by short-waisted, double- or single-breasted coats with long tails behind, showing the full length of skin-tight pantaloons from waist to ankle. Extremely fastidious gentlemen were obliged to remain standing so as not to disturb their creaseless appearance. With this body-hugging attire, the emphasis on a 'fine leg' was such that false calves were intro-duced to achieve the correct curvature. The neck was swathed in wide cra-vats surrounded by immensely high collars that came up to the cheeks. The tricorn hat, which had been fashionable for a century, was replaced by round hats with broad brims and either a low, round or a high, tapered crown.

Most young men and some women had their hair cut and arranged in short curls around the face, a style criticized by Jane Austen, among others, who disapproved of her niece Anna's 'bobbed' head. Writing in 1793 of what he called the 'era of Jacobinism' in London, Sir Nathaniel Wraxall observed: 'it was then that pantaloons, cropped hair, and shoe-strings as well as the total abolition of buckles and ruffles, together with the disuse of hair powder, characterised men; while the ladies, having cut off those tresses which had done so much execution, exhibited heads rounded *à la victime et à la guillotine*, as if ready for the stroke of the axe.'

By the turn of the century, the stiffness and formality that had once characterized fashion had completely disappeared, replaced by the softer, column-like shape of the Regency style. For the next decade or more the vogue was for only the simplest styles in pale colours, with only delicate decoration permitted. Soft white muslins were woven or embroidered with tiny spots or floral sprigs scattered over the ground or confined to borders. Dresses with trains were worn for both day and evening from 1800 to 1806. Oliver Goldsmith commented:

> what chiefly distinguishes the sex at present is the train. As a lady's quality or fashion was once determined here by the circumference of her hoop, both are now measured by the length of her tail. Women of moderate fortunes are contented with tails moderately long but ladies of true taste and distinction set no bounds to their ambition in this particular.

In *Northanger Abbey* Isabella Thorpe and Catherine Morland 'pinned up each other's train for the dance'. The length of the trains is left to the reader's imagination, but one suspects that Isabella, a social climber, would allow hers to be somewhat longer than that of the more timid Catherine.

Regency style for men was associated with Beau Brummell, that Napoleon of style and arbiter of manners who distinguished country clothes by giving hunting dress the immaculate, well-tailored appearance that became standard for the next twenty years, and endured, indeed, with few exceptions, to the present day. A coat for men specifically mentioned in the novels is the 'great coat', a large, loose-fitting overcoat reaching below the knee, with one or more broad collars or capes. These were commonly used for travelling and were very practical when the weather was inclement. In *Northanger Abbey* Mrs Allen remarks: 'I hope Mr Allen will put on his great coat when he goes, but I dare say he will not, for he had rather do anything in the world than walk out in the great coat; I wonder he should dislike it. It must be so comfortable'. After 1815 the frock coat, dissimilar from the earlier coat of the same name, replaced the tail coat for day wear. It was distinguished by straight-cut front edges that overlapped, rather than being cut away, and was worn with trousers in either a matching or contrasting material – a hint of the style worn by gentlemen today.

After 1810 women's dresses received more emphasis on the sleeve and more decoration on the bodice. The waistline very gradually began to drop, and heavier ornamentation was arranged around the hem, which eventually encouraged the widening of the skirt. 'I wear my gauze gown

*Beau Brummell, who set the pace in terms of fashionable style for men during the Regency period – from a miniature by John Cooke. The exaggerated fastidiousness he popularized was often mocked by caricaturists such as Cruickshank. Right: 'A Fashionable of 1817'.*

today,' Jane Austen wrote in March 1814, 'long sleeves & all; I shall see how they succeed, but as yet I have no reason to suppose long sleeves are allowable'; but she goes on to say: 'Mrs. Tilson had long sleeves too, & she assured me that they are worn in the evening by many. I was glad to hear this.' In September of the same year she wrote from London that 'Long sleeves appear universal, even as *Dress*, the Waists short, and as far as I have been able to judge, the Bosom covered.'

Over their dresses ladies wore spencers or pelisses. The spencer was a short jacket of wool or silk, cut like the bodice, usually with long sleeves and a high neck, while the pelisse was a coat cut in a line complementary to the dress. In *Mansfield Park*, when Fanny Price visited Portsmouth she was not considered worthy of the notice of the young ladies there, for 'she neither played on the piano forte nor wore fine pelisses'.

As the century progressed, ladies' fashions became increasingly structured, to the point of virtual bondage during the Victorian era. Unlike the gentlemen, ladies have been allowed more variety in their finery, so their attire has undergone more or less constant change until the present day.

## The following of fashion

Before the Revolution, those unable to visit Paris to view the latest fashions kept current of changing styles by receiving French 'fashion babies' (pattern-dressed dolls), which were sent regularly from Paris to London. Laetitia Powell preserved past fashions by collecting samples of her wardrobe, with which she dressed twenty-three dolls between 1754 and 1832, labelling each one with the style it was wearing. Fashions worn at assembly balls and other social gatherings were noted and sketched out later, to be shared with friends and relatives, or perhaps the dressmaker. The Shelburne Museum in Vermont, USA, has a collection of forty-nine sketches of fashionable clothes made between 1784 and 1805 by an unknown amateur artist. Professional artists could boost their earnings by producing fashion plates for such periodicals as *La Belle Assemblée*, *Ackerman's Repository* or the *Lady's Magazine*. Pocket books had fold-out engravings of the latest styles, often depicted in a theatrical setting. Fanny Austen Knight's pocket book of 1805 shows fashionable ladies caught in the Gothic drama of *Lussington Abbey*. Fanny carefully cut out their paper clothes, leaving faces and arms, and placed swatches of silk and muslin behind the engravings where the costumes had been, so dressing the figures with real textiles.

But news of the latest fashions was generally spread by word of mouth and through letters. In *Pride and Prejudice* Mrs Gardiner's first duty upon her arrival to stay with the Bennets 'was to distribute her presents and describe the newest fashions', and when Jane Bennet returns home from a visit with friends, 'Mrs Bennet was doubly engaged, on one hand collecting an account of the present fashions from Jane, who sat some way below her, and on the other, relating them all to the younger Miss Lucases.' In her letter of 1814 Jane Austen reported on the London fashions to her friend Martha Lloyd: 'I am amused by the present style of female dress; the coloured petticoats with braces over the white Spencers and enormous Bonnets upon the full stretch, are quite entertaining. It seems to me a

*Ball Dress.*     *Afternoon Dress.*     *Morning Dress.*

*Ball dress, afternoon dress and morning dress for 1808, from a pocket book belonging to Fanny Austen Knight. Ladies often made their own sketches of fashions they had seen worn at concerts, assembly balls and other social gatherings. This anonymous drawing* (opposite) *is one of forty-nine sketches of fashionable gowns, made between 1784 and 1805, now in the Shelburne Museum, Vermont.*

more marked *change* than one has lately seen.' Fanny Austen Knight was even more descriptive when relating news of the ensembles worn by herself and three young ladies who accompanied her to the Canterbury balls:

> We wore white crepe dresses trimmed with satin ribbon & the bodices & sleeves spotted with white beads, over satin petticoats, the Thursday night, Pearl combs, necklaces, earrings & brooches. We had a hairdresser from town for the week & were all four alike every night. Tuesday evening we had sprigged muslin trimmed with Broad lace over satin slips, gold ornaments & flowers in our heads, & Friday we wore yellow gauze dresses over satin, beads in our heads & pearl ornaments.

Newspapers, though their circulation figures were not large – 2000 was high, and *The Times* in 1795 reached only 4800 – were passed on from reader to reader, and offered a good source of information on current fashions. From the *London Recorder*, 1806: 'The dresses of ladies were in general white muslin, with a slight intermixture of lilac and peach blossom. The head-dresses were either Grecian or Egyptian; ostrich feathers were generally worn: on the whole the Drawing-room wore a much more brilliant aspect than usual.'

The fact that dress was an indicator of one's fortune and status compelled the money-oriented society of the Georgian era to indulge in considerable expenditure in order to keep abreast of the latest fashions. Rapid inflation caused by the French wars – over 100 per cent in the 1790s – was particularly distressing for those on fixed incomes, and yet foreigners visiting London marvelled at finding people of all classes – servants and nobles alike – finely attired in the latest styles. A character in Mary Meeke's novel *Conscience* (1814) declared in outrage, 'now every petty clerk sports boots, pantaloons, jackets, and bang-up great coats; and spends more in clothes in one year than he earns in two.' In spite of high inflation this was a period of almost rampant consumerism. The Industrial Revolution brought wealth to a broader spectrum of society, which now included manufacturers, industrialists and their families, and created more products, which were more readily available and at a greater variety of costs.

Jane Austen was both a participant in, and a victim of this spending mania; writing from London in 1811, she said: 'We set off immediately after breakfast & must have reached Grafton House by ¹/₂ past 11 –, but when we entered the Shop, the whole Counter was thronged, & we waited *full* half an hour before we cᵈ be attended to. When we were served however, I was very well satisfied with my purchases'. Grafton House was a linen-draper's shop, where dress fabrics, trimmings and the materials for dress accessories could be purchased. Friends or relations visiting London were often commissioned to make purchases for those left at home, and in the same letter of 1811 Jane wrote,

I am sorry to tell you that I am getting very extravagant & spending
all my Money; & what is worse for *you*, I have been spending yours
too; for in a Linendraper's shop to which I went for check'd muslin, &
for which I was obliged to give seven shillings a yard, I was tempted
by a pretty coloured muslin, & bought 10 y$^{ds}$ of it, on the chance of
your liking it; – but at the same time if it sh$^d$ not suit you, you must not
think yourself at all obliged to take it; it is only 3/6 p$^r$ y$^d$, & I sh$^d$ not in
the least mind keeping the whole. – In texture, it is just what we prefer,
but it's resemblance to green cruels I must own is not great, for the
pattern is a small red spot. . . . & now I believe I have done all my commissions, except Wedgwood.

Although London and Bath were considered shopping Meccas by
country dwellers, with improved roads and transport country towns and
villages once 'sadly off' in the range of merchandise offered for sale
increasingly enhanced their selection of goods. There were also the annual
country fairs, which attracted huge crowds, and traders offering fabrics
and trimmings among hundreds of other products. If these outlets failed,
door-to-door pedlars occasionally proffered articles worth having.

*In spite of the sharp inflation of the French war years from 1793 to 1815, shopping for fabrics and fashions remained one of the main attractions of towns like London and Bath. Jane wrote to Cassandra in 1811, 'I am getting very extravagant and spending all my Money'. Right: Walking dress, 1819. After 1810, greater emphasis was laid on the sleeves and hem.*

The fluidity of ladies' fashions demanded lightweight materials. Muslin was the most popular fabric for gowns and the one most frequently mentioned by Jane Austen in both the novels and letters. The term muslin covered many varieties of fine, delicately woven cotton in a range of colours, but white was the most popular, especially for evening wear. The very elegant Eleanor Tilney (*Northanger Abbey*) always wore white, and in *Mansfield Park*, when Fanny Price is worried about appearing over-dressed in a white gown, her cousin Edmund Bertram assures her, 'a woman can never be too fine while she is all in white.' Muslin, white or otherwise, was a useful textile for other items, such as neckerchiefs, pocket handkerchiefs, caps, aprons, shawls and veils. Even Henry Tilney appreciated its versatility: 'Muslin always tends to some account or other; Miss Morland will get enough of it for a handkerchief or a cap, or a cloak. – Muslin can never be said to be wasted.' Other popular fashion textiles included sarcenet, a silk that was less tightly woven than other silks and therefore draped easily, which made it suitable for gowns as well as lining; lawn or long lawn, which was a very fine linen, and cambric, a fine, plain white linen used for shirts and ladies' summer wear; holland became the generic term for fine linen cloth, and in its lighter quality was fashionable for men's shirts. Heavier linens, such Irish linen, and cottons, such as calico or dimity, were also used.

For day wear, coloured gowns were most practical. In 1801 Jane wrote,

> I shall want two new coloured gowns for the summer, for my pink one will not do more than clear me from Steventon. I shall not trouble you, however, to get more than one of them, and that is to be a plain brown cambric muslin, for morning wear; the other, which is to be a very pretty yellow and white cloud, I mean to buy in Bath.

Isabella Thorpe, in *Northanger Abbey*, announced to Catherine Morland: 'I wear nothing but purple now: I know I look hideous in it, but no matter – it is your dear brother's favourite colour.' A certain Miss Fletcher 'wore her purple Muslin, which is pretty enough, tho' it does not become her complexion', according to Jane Austen in 1796. Women's clothes were frequently dyed during this period to provide a change of colour, to convert gowns to mourning, or perhaps to restore colour that had been washed out. In 1796 Jane Austen wrote: 'I am sorry to say that my new coloured gown is very much washed out, though I charged everybody to take great care of it.' Garments were often ruined in the process of dyeing, however. In 1808 Jane wrote to her sister, 'how is your blue gown? – Mine is all to peices. – I think there must have been something wrong in the dye, for in places it divided with a Touch. – There was four shillings thrown away; – to be added to my subjects of never failing regret.'

The plainer gowns provided a background for embellishment with embroidery or various trimmings. The fashion- and status-seeking Mrs Elton in *Emma* asks, 'How do you like my gown? How do you like my trimming!' Ribbon trimming or edging was fashionable in 1813 when Jane Austen wrote, 'my gown is to be trimmed everywhere with white ribbon plaited somehow or other'. A year later she wrote, 'I have determined to trim my lilac sarsenet with black sattin ribbon. . . . Ribbon trimmings are all the fashion at Bath'. Further on in the letter she adds, 'I have been ruining myself in black sattin ribbon with a proper perl edge; & now I am trying to draw it up into kind of roses, instead of putting it in plain double plaits.' Another popular trimming was made of tubular-shaped glass bugle beads. In 1811 Jane Austen bought bugle trimming at 2/4d. and wore a band of it on her head to match the border on her gown.

Having purchased fabric and trimmings for a gown, pelisse or other garment, the next step was to consult with the dressmaker. Some printed patterns were available, but more often patterns were made from the components of other gowns. Either way, instructions to the dressmaker needed to be explicit with regard to design and stylistic details. Isabella Thorpe (*Northanger Abbey*) was rather proud of her creation: 'How do you like my gown? I think it does not look amiss; the sleeves were entirely my own thought.' During the eighteenth century the seamstress who made women's gowns was known as a 'mantua-maker', a mantua being a type of gown fashionable at the end of the seventeenth century. The term continued in use until the middle of the nineteenth century. In the cancelled chapter of *Persuasion*, Admiral Croft urges Anne Elliot to visit his wife and assures her that she is "'quite alone, nobody but her mantua-maker with her, and they have been shut up together this half-hour, so it must be over soon." "Her mantua-maker! Then I am sure my calling now would be most inconvenient."' The letters contain references to frequent visits by Jane Austen to various dressmakers. In 1811 a Miss Burton made pelisses for Jane and her sister: 'Our Pelisses are 17/s. each –', she wrote; 'she charges only 8/ for the making, but the Buttons seem expensive'.

One of the skills that distinguished a ladies' maid from other female members of the household staff was her talent for needlework. In addition to making decorative domestic items, it was her office to repair her lady's garments and, if her ability allowed, to make up new gowns for her mistress. At Mansfield Park Lady Bertram's maid 'was rather hurried in making up a new dress for her'. The making, altering and repairing of clothes at home was not restricted to servants, however. All gentlewomen occupied some portion of the day or week with needlework, and for many this pastime included sewing gowns and their accessories, shirts, cravats, caps, stockings, children's and babies' clothes. Writing to Cassandra at Godmersham Park in 1809, Jane Austen commented, 'I can easily suppose that your six weeks here will be fully occupied, were it only in lengthening the waist of your gowns.' In *Northanger Abbey* Henry Tilney chides his sister's extravagance in purchasing more muslin 'than she wanted' or carelessly 'cutting it to pieces'. James Edward Austen-Leigh recalled in his *Memoir* of his aunt that 'some of her merriest talk was of the clothes which she and her companions were making, sometimes for themselves and sometimes for the poor.'

## *The finishing touches*

Hundreds of accessories were available to wear with dresses and became indispensable with the simple Regency styles. Not the least of these was the shawl. Lady Bertram in *Mansfield Park* was anxious to have a shawl from the East: 'William must not forget my shawl, if he goes to the East Indies; and I shall give him a commission for anything else that is worth having. I wish he may go to the East Indies, that I may have my shawl. I think I will have two shawls'. Indian shawls of cashmere were popular and were later copied by British textile manufacturers. The fashion had originally been for an oblong shape, but later tended towards the square. Shawls were also made of lighter materials to complement the dresses they were accompanying. Jane Austen mentions in a letter of 1805, 'Mary Whitby's turn is actually come to be grown up & have a fine complexion & wear great square muslin shawls.'

Cloaks were often more decorative than functional and made of light material; 'Black gauze cloaks are worn as much as anything', wrote Jane in a letter of 1801. In 1812 she bought a cloak of grey wool at a cost of ten shillings. Decorative, long, cylindrical fur tippets were also worn over the shoulders for day and evening wear; 'You cannot think how much my Ermine Tippet is admired both by Father & Daughter', Jane wrote to her sister in 1814. (Her admirers were Edward and Fanny Austen Knight.)

Hats were customarily worn out of doors, and caps were worn indoors by married women and single women of advancing years; Jane Austen donned the cap from the early age of twenty-three. Caroline Austen, writing about her aunt, recalled that 'She always wore a cap – Such was the custom with the ladies who were not quite young – at least of a morning – but I never saw her without one, to the best of my remembrance, either morning or evening.' In 1798 Jane wrote to her sister: 'I have made myself two or three caps to wear of evenings since I came home, and they save me a world of torment as to hair-dressing'. Happily, her matron-like attitude toward caps did not extend to bonnets, and like most women of the period she revealed a more frivolous nature in the choice and design of these items. Toward the end of the eighteenth century the fashion was for trimming hats with artificial flowers and fruit. Hats were altered to meet with the changing styles, or were purchased from the milliner unadorned and later decorated by the wearer. In 1799 Jane wrote to Cassandra,

> Flowers are very much worn, & Fruit is still more the thing. Eliz: has a bunch of Strawberries, & I have seen Grapes, Cherries, Plumbs & Apricots – There are likewise Almonds & raisins, french plumbs & Tamarinds at the Grocers, but I have never seen any of them in hats. – A plumb or greengage would cost three shillings; – Cherries & grapes about 5 I beleive – but this is at some of the dearest shops; – My aunt has told me of a very cheap one near Walcot Church, to which I shall go in quest of something for you.

Bonnets and caps were also trimmed with lace or brightly coloured ribbons, such as the poppy red 'coquelicot'. In *Northanger Abbey* Isabella Thorpe tells Catherine Morland: 'Do you know, I saw the prettiest hat you can imagine, in a shop window in Milsom-street just now – very like yours, only with coquelicot ribbons instead of green; I quite longed for it.' For evening wear caps were given extra verve, like the one Jane Austen was altering in December 1798: 'I still venture to retain the narrow silver round it, put twice round without any bow, & instead of the black military feather shall put in the Coquelicot one, as being smarter; – & besides Coquelicot is to be all the fashion this winter. – After the Ball, I shall probably make it entirely black.' But a little later she added, 'I have changed my mind & changed the trimmings of my Cap this morning; they are now such as you suggested; – I felt as if I should not prosper if I strayed from your directions.' Another cap mentioned in the letters is the 'Mamalone', probably a misreading for 'Mamalouc'. Following the Battle of the Nile in 1798, the rage was for Mamalouc (or Mameluk) caps, robes and cloaks. This 'cap' was actually a turban trimmed with an ostrich feather.

Bonnets were made of a variety of materials in addition to straw (strip or chip), such as beaver, velvet, satin, silk or muslin:

*Early nineteenth-century bonnets from the* Repository of the Arts. *Great attention was paid to head-wear, with flowers, fruit, ribbon and lace being the most popular trimmings.*

My mother has ordered a new bonnet, and so have I; both white strip, trimmed with white ribbon. I find my straw bonnet looking very much like other people's, and quite as smart. Bonnets of cambric muslin on the plan of Lady Bridges' are a good deal worn, and some of them are very pretty; but I shall defer one of that sort till your arrival.

Veils were often worn with bonnets: 'I watched for *veils* as we drove through the streets, and had the pleasure of seeing several upon vulgar heads', wrote Jane from London in 1814, and Tom Bertram in *Mansfield Park* refers to two young ladies of his acquaintance being 'both well dressed, with veils and parasols like other girls'. Mr Bertram's 'young ladies' were at Ramsgate and particularly well protected, it appears, from the coastal sunshine, as they had both veils and gaily coloured silk parasols. Parasols often matched gowns or pelisses in colour and material and were very fashionable in the summer. In May 1801 Jane Austen, out for a walk in Bath with a friend, was concerned that her friend should be 'without any parasol or any shade to her hat'. It was not until the early nineteenth century that gentlemen protected themselves from the weather by the use of umbrellas. These were silver-framed and covered with fancy blue or green silk. They were aristocratically held firmly by the middle, with the carved ivory, gold, silver or stag's horn handle pointing towards the ground. In *Persuasion* Captain Wentworth tells Anne Elliot, 'though I came only yesterday, I have equipped myself properly for Bath already, you see [pointing to a new umbrella]'.

Beneath the headdresses of the Regency period, hair was generally worn in a short, natural style, or short at the front with curls about the face, leaving the back hair long enough to be drawn up to the crown of the head in a chignon and fastened with combs. Curls were created by twisting the tresses around paper. Most ladies had their hair dressed by a maid or professional hairdresser. Whilst staying at Godmersham Park, Jane Austen had her hair dressed by a Mr Hall, who came to the house to attend both Jane and her sister-in-law Elizabeth, and to give the latter's maid instructions in the art of coiffure. 'M^r Hall', she reported to Cassandra '... charged Eliz^th 5s. for every time of dressing her hair, & 5s. for every lesson to Sace.... Towards me he was as considerate, as I had hoped for, ... charging me only 2s. 6d. for cutting my hair, tho' it was as thoroughly dress'd after being cut for Eastwell, as it had been for the Ashford Assembly.' Some years later, in September 1813, she again mentioned Mr Hall, who 'was very punctual yesterday, and curled me out at a great rate. I thought it looked hideous, and longed for a snug cap instead, but my companions silenced me by their admiration. I had only a bit of velvet round my head. I did not catch cold however.'

Ladies' shoes, for day and evening wear, were of the simple slipper type and came in a variety of colours and patterns, often made to match specific garments; green, pink, white and black shoes are mentioned by Jane Austen, while blue shoes appear in 'William Heeley's windows' in *Sanditon*. Indoor shoes were constructed of leather, and also of silk and satin; they were purchased ready-made or specially ordered to measure. Lord Osborne in *The Watsons* begged 'that his Sister might be allow'd to send Emma the name of her Shoemaker', and in *Mansfield Park* Mary Crawford tells Fanny Price that her friend 'will be at me for ever about your eyes and your teeth, and how you do your hair, and who makes your shoes'. Half-boots, possibly made of nankeen – a heavy yellow cotton cloth named after its place of origin, Nanking in China – were worn for walking and riding. In *Emma* Miss Woodhouse tactfully falls behind her two companions to adjust the lacings of her half-boot:

> She then broke the lace off short, and dexterously throwing it into a ditch, was presently obliged to entreat them to stop and acknowledge her inability to put herself to rights so as to be able to walk home in tolerable comfort. 'Part of my lace is gone . . . Mr Elton, I must beg leave to stop at your house, and ask your housekeeper for a bit of ribband or string, or anything just to keep my boot on.'

To raise the wearer above muddy streets and pathways, pattens were worn. These were overshoes with wooden soles supported on iron rings; among the cacophonous sounds of Bath that Anne Elliot found distressing was 'the ceaseless clink of pattens' (*Persuasion*). Pattens were also worn by kitchen- or housemaids when washing floors.

*A visit to the shoe-maker's, c.1820. Slipper-type shoes would have been available in a variety of colours to correspond with the pattern or colour of gowns, and were therefore important accessories. Ladies took great care in choosing their 'Shoemaker'.*

Muffs and gloves were worn by both ladies and gentlemen. Muffs came in winter and summer weights, the winter weight being of fur and the summer weight of swansdown or feathers. In the eighteenth century muffs were very large, but they became smaller in size in the nineteenth century. Gloves were an important dress accessory, particularly for evening wear, and were made of leather, silk, or could be hand-knitted. In 1798 Jane wrote to her sister, 'I have unpacked the gloves and placed yours in your drawer. Their colour is light and pretty, and I believe exactly what we fixed on'; and in 1813 she was pleased with her purchase of gloves:

> I was very lucky in my gloves – got them at the first shop I went to, though I went into it rather because it was near than because it looked at all like a glove shop, and gave only four shillings for them; upon hearing which everybody at Chawton will be hoping and predicting that they cannot be good for anything, and their worth certainly remains to be proved; but I think they look very well.

Another indispensable fashion accessory for ladies was the fan. The manipulation of a fan could express a whole spectrum of emotions – words were scarcely necessary – though it was said to take three months before the art of 'fluttering' was fully mastered. The more expensive fans were mounted with diamonds and inlaid with jewels, and were painted with political emblems, verses from popular songs, poetry, battle scenes, birds, cherubs, flowers and fruit.

A lady's necessities, such as a fan, scent bottle and handkerchief, were carried in a small bag, or reticule, which was often circular or losenge-shaped. Mrs Elton in *Emma* had a purple and gold reticule in which she had carried a letter. For carrying coins, a popular purse was the 'stocking', or 'miser's purse'; long and narrow in shape, with an opening in the centre, it had two rings to close it and ornaments at either end. Many of these were knitted, netted or crocheted, and making purses was a popular pastime; Mr Bingley in *Pride and Prejudice* considered netting a purse a female 'accomplishment'.

Jewelry was worn to a minimum, if at all, during the day, all the glitter being reserved for evening dress. Styles of jewelry evolved with the style of clothes, though less rapidly, with fashionable dress materials – such as silks and gauzes – or the neckline of the bodice determining chain length and construction. Settings were frequently altered to bring them into line with contemporary designs and the latest dress styles, as with the late eighteenth-century hair ornaments, which were converted into brooches in the early nineteenth century. Between 1806 and 1807 *La Belle Assemblée* recorded 'brooches for the bosom and throat', 'brooches on the head with comb' and 'brooches for looping up sleeves'. In *Emma*, Frank Churchill is delighted that his fiancée is to be given all his aunt's jewels: 'they are to be new set. I am resolved to have some in an ornament for the head. Will it not be beautiful in her dark hair?' Jewels for the hair were very popular during this era. The June 1808 issue of *La Belle Assemblée* stated that: 'The ornaments worn on the hair are alternately of diamonds, pearl or polished

*A late eighteenth-century trade card for Newman, 'Goldsmith and Jeweller' in London, offering 'Rings and Jewels of the neatest and most fashionable Taste'.*

steel. Combs and coronets of silver filigree, bandeaus of pearl, with the pear drop in the centre of the forehead, tiaras and wreaths of flowers.' In *Northanger Abbey* Eleanor Tilney is seen at a ball with 'white beads round her head'.

Pearls were costly and therefore reserved for the adornment of the upper classes or the nouveaux riches. Mrs Elton, in *Emma*, is delighted to announce, 'I see very few pearls in the room except mine', while in *Northanger Abbey* 'there was a very beautiful set of pearls that Miss Tilney had got now, for they were put by for her when her mother died'. Crosses were popular in Latin, Greek and Maltese forms. Jane and Cassandra Austen were given topaz crosses on gold chains by their brother Charles in 1801. Fanny Price, in *Mansfield Park*, receives an amber cross from her brother, though the matter of the chain gives her some perplexity. She originally intends wearing her cross on a ribbon, but for her first ball feels the ribbon may be inappropriate 'in the midst of all the rich ornaments which she supposed all the other young ladies would appear in'. Mary Crawford gives Fanny a 'prettily worked' gold chain, which unfortunately is too thick for the ring of the cross. But catastrophe is avoided with the present of a 'plain gold chain, perfectly simple and neat', from Edmund Bertram, Fanny's cousin. At the ball she wears both to cause no offence.

Rings were worn by men and women, then as now, as symbols of loyalty or allegiance – such as the one worn by Edward Ferrars in *Sense and Sensibility*. Fanny Austen Knight and her friend Miss Chapman exchanged rings made of each other's hair, and the hair of a loved one was also worn encased in a locket for remembrance. Decorative buckles were worn by men in evening dress for fastening shoe straps and the straps at the outer knees of their breeches. They were also used to secure men's neckcloth or stock at the nape of the neck.

The development of imitation gemstones and precious metals was evident during the Regency period. Colourless paste jewelry complemented neo-classical dresses, which favoured white, and as coloured embroidery outwear and accessories appeared, so too did coloured pastes reflecting the palette of the silk-dyers of the period.

Jane Austen chose a real jeweler's shop, Gray's in Sackville Street, London, for a scene in *Sense and Sensibility*: 'Elinor was carrying on a negotiation for the exchange of a few old-fashioned jewels of her mother'. Her brother, Mr John Dashwood, meets Elinor there by chance, but carefully explains his financial position in order 'to do away with the necessity of buying a pair of earrings for each of his sisters on his next visit at Gray's'. Bits and bobs, trinkets and ornaments, could also be purchased at circulating libraries during the eighteenth and nineteenth centuries. In *Sanditon* Charlotte Heywood goes 'to buy new Parasols, new Gloves & new Brooches, for her sisters and herself at the Library'. There she finds a number of tempting items but wisely 'turned from the Drawers of rings & Brooches, repressed further solicitation & paid for what she bought'. Lydia Bennet in *Pride and Prejudice* writes to her family that she has just been to the library, 'where she had seen such beautiful ornaments as made her quite wild'.

Beneath the tubular dress styles of the period a simple shift or chemise made of linen replaced form-hugging buckskin. Jane Austen bought six shifts from a travelling salesman in November 1798. New or second-hand shifts were also given to the servants and the local poor by the Austen ladies. As the century progressed, drawers – separate legs attached to a waistband – were worn. Stays began to shrink in size at the end of the eighteenth century as the bodice of the dress shortened. Some women dispensed with stays altogether, while others altered them to suit the changing fashions. In September 1813 Jane noted: 'I learnt from Mrs. Tickars's young lady, to my high amusement, that the stays now are not made to force the bosom up at all; *that* was a very unbecoming, unnatural fashion. I was really glad to hear that they are not to be so much off the shoulders as they were'. Stays were worn with shoulder straps at this stage, whereas the plunging necklines of the first decade of the century had not always been able to accommodate stays with shoulder straps. From Bath in 1801 Jane Austen wrote, 'Miss Langley is like any other short girl with a broad nose & wide mouth, fashionable dress, & exposed bosom.'

Stockings were the subject of much discussion in the letters and a particular weakness of Jane's. She admitted preferring to have only two pairs of fine quality to three of an inferior sort. The best were made of silk, and in 1811 three pairs could be purchased 'for a little less than 12/s. a pᵣ'. In September 1813 Fanny Austen Knight was 'very much pleased with the stockings she has bought of Remmington – Silk at 12/s. – Cotton at 4/3d. – She thinks them great bargains'. Stockings were generally white or flesh-coloured and held in place with garters. They were also made of wool, though the worsted ones to which Jane refers were given to the needy; these were practical and warm, but certainly not elegant. Jane Fairfax, in *Emma*, knits a pair for her grandmother.

## *Enhancing nature's gifts: cosmetics and cleanliness*

During the eighteenth century women poisoned their bodies and damaged their skin by painting the face, arms and *décolletage* with ceruse, containing white lead. Pock marks and facial ulcers were hidden behind face patches in the shape of hearts or crescents. Patching for both men and women remained popular until about 1790, though by this time stark white faces with reddened lips and cheeks were passing out of fashion. Faces during the Regency period were admired for a naturally pale beauty and clear complexion, though some older women maintained the blush of youth with the help of a little rouge. Sir Walter Elliot in *Persuasion* felt that the elderly Lady Russell might benefit from this: 'morning visits are never fair by women at her time of life, who make themselves up so little. If only she would wear rouge, she would not be afraid of being seen.' While attending a ball at the Bath assembly rooms in 1801, Jane Austen spied a supposed adulteress whom she thought was 'highly rouged, & looked rather quietly & contentedly silly than anything else.' The Prince Regent suffered from the reverse complaint; his complexion was too florid, for which he regularly applied leeches, followed by a liberal dusting of face powder.

Sir Walter Elliot also felt that freckles were rather disfiguring; on his recommendation, Mrs Clay used Gowland's Lotion, and he was convinced of its success. Gowland's Lotion, a real product, was sold widely at this time, and was described in an advertisement of 1814 as 'the most pleasant and effective remedy for all complaints to which the Face and Skin are liable'. Sir Walter found it hard to believe that his daughter's improved looks were not the result of her using Gowland's Lotion; he thought her 'less thin in her person, in her cheeks; her skin, her complexion, greatly improved – clearer, fresher. Had she been using anything in particular? "No, nothing." "Merely Gowland", he supposed. "No, nothing at all." "Ha! he was surprised at that," and added, "Certainly you cannot do better than continue as you are; you cannot be better than well; or I should recommend Gowland, the constant use of Gowland, during the spring months."'

There were also numerous commercial products available for whitening the teeth, supplemented by home remedies for tooth complaints. Toothache was the most common medical complaint of the period. The most common solution was extraction, but teeth were also hand-drilled and filled with molten lead, tin or gold. In 1800 Wedgwood supplied paste for the making of china teeth. The prevalence of advertisements and the bustling trade in tooth removal suggest a lot of imperfect smiles.

**These ladies** are from Fanny Austen Knight's pocket book of 1805. Fanny carefully cut out their paper costumes and placed swatches of silk and muslin behind the engravings, so that the figures display not only the latest fashionable gowns, but also the latest fabrics. Fanny would doubtless have spent many hours learning the delicate art of manipulating a fan. This example, handpainted with a motif celebrating a British military victory, may have belonged to Mrs Austen.

For most, personal cleanliness was limited to a daily washing of the hands and face, and a bath only every few weeks or months. Still, this was an improvement on the early eighteenth century, when overall bathing was considered to be positively dangerous to one's health; it was during the early eighteenth century that perfume had been used in abundance by men and women to mask offensive odours. By the nineteenth century the fashion was for lighter scent, such as the 'sweet waters' of lavender, orange-flower, rose or honey. In 1801 Jane asked Cassandra to buy a friend 'two bottles of Steele's Lavender Water when you are in Town'. One of Brummell's decrees was that no gentleman should ever use perfume, but should send his linen to be washed and dried on Hampstead Heath in North London. The French took this dictum so seriously, that those who could afford it sent their linen to England to be laundered! However, George IV continued to use perfume: in 1822 his perfume bill was £263 and six years later it had almost doubled. Brummell also had very particular notions about bathing; his aversion to dirt obliged him to bathe three or four times a day. Even the soles of his boots were polished – perhaps with a mixture of boot black and champagne, as he recommended to one young gentleman. Thus, scrupulous cleanliness became the fashion among Regency dandies, who lived in horror of being caught with a speck of dust upon their highly polished boots or lint on a coat.

This new fashion for cleanliness may partly have contributed to the popularity of lightweight cottons and pale muslins that could be easily washed. But while these fabrics responded well to washing, they tended to be somewhat fragile. In *Northanger Abbey* Catherine Morland is teased by Henry Tilney when he admires her gown, but says: 'I do not think it will wash well; I'm afraid it will fray.'

## Dress for every occasion

The special types of occupational or ceremonial dress Jane Austen is most likely to have seen are mourning dress, military uniforms, the livery of male servants, and wedding clothes – probably in that order of frequency.

Mourning was strictly observed during this time, for public figures such as members of the royal family, as well as for friends and relatives – even distant relatives. Given that families were very large, men and women were frequently obliged to wear black. Brown, though less usual, was also acceptable for mourning, and for second-mourning or half-mourning, worn before returning to normal wear, lighter colours trimmed with black were permitted. The favourite fabrics for mourning clothes were bombazine, crêpe and cotton, as well as velvet. Bombazine had a silk warp and woollen weft, and crêpe was an appropriate silk for mourning as it had a matt surface, as opposed to the sheen of other silks. It was not uncommon to have garments dyed for the purpose of mourning: 'My Mother is preparing mourning for Mrs. E.K. – she has picked her old silk

*Dashing uniformed gentlemen such as these would have set many a young lady's heart a-flutter. Left: An officer of the 95th Foot Regiment, c.1800. Right: Officer of the 7th Light Dragoons, c.1793.*

pelisse to peices, & means to have it dyed black for a gown – a very interesting scheme'. Jane herself was to be

> in bombazeen and crape, according to what we are told is universal *here*, and which agrees with Martha's previous observation. My mourning, however, will not impoverish me, for by having my velvet pelisse fresh lined and made up, I am sure I shall have no occasion *this winter* for anything new of that sort. I take my cloak for the lining, and shall send yours on the chance of its doing something of the same for you, though I believe your pelisse is in better repair than mine. *One* Miss Baker makes my gown and the other my bonnet, which is to be silk covered with crape.

Jane Austen also took on the task of choosing mourning dress for two of her nephews, Edward and George, after the death of their mother: 'Edward has an old black coat, which will save *his* having a second new one; but I find that black pantaloons are considered by them as necessary, and of course one would not have them made uncomfortable by the want of what is usual on such occasions.'

It seems that men in uniform possessed a unique charm much appreciated by ladies. Mrs Austen admired them, while Lydia Bennet in *Pride and Prejudice* found them positively irresistible. Fanny Austen Knight, writing from Godmersham Park to her friend in 1804, said 'Captain [Charles] Austen looks very nice in his red coat, Blue breeches & red Sash, he is now sitting opposite to me & I can hardly write my letter for looking at him. The hat is a plain round common one with an oak bough & a crescent in the middle.' With the Napoleonic Wars, ladies would have found plenty of opportunities to observe such smartly dressed young men, and with three brothers in the service of their country, Jane no doubt encountered several uniformed representatives of His Majesty's forces.

*An **Evening** dress* in the style of the late eighteenth century, kid gloves and a black ostrich feather for the hair.

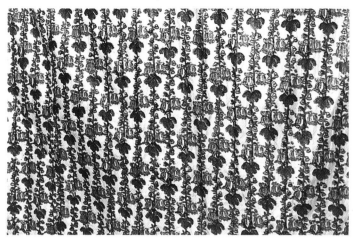

*Flowers, ribbons, jewels, strips of muslin, caps and feathers were all popular as evening hair accessories for ladies, and much thought was given to the overall effect. Printed fabrics of the period reveal a rich variety of design: a cotton dress fabric* (above) *and a block-printed chintz* (below) *of the 1790s.*

Male servants tended to wear specific garments at different times of the day and special uniforms according to their office. The most lavish of these was the livery worn by footmen and postilions – the grander the better, as it was an obvious indication of their master's wealth and status; footmen took pride in out-dressing staff from neighbouring households. The uniform called for well-powdered, well-dressed and neatly tied hair or a wig, a brightly coloured coat with numerous polished buttons, knee breeches and stockings. Sir Walter Elliot, in *Persuasion*, remarks that Admiral Croft's weather-beaten face is 'about as orange as the cuffs and capes of my livery', while Fanny Austen Knight's future husband, Sir Edward Knatchbull, kept his servants in blue livery. The Tilneys (*Northanger Abbey*) travel with 'postilions handsomely liveried', and visitors to the Edwards family in *The Watsons* are greeted at the door by a 'Man Livery with a powder'd head'. Originally this form of dress was worn by the servants of an important household or individual so that they might be immediately recognizable in the street. In *Persuasion*, Mary Musgrove fails to notice William Elliot and his servant at Lyme because they are in mourning: 'I am sure, I should have observed them, and the livery too; if the servant had not been in mourning one should have known him by the livery.' For most well-to-do families the expenditure on livery for possibly as many as twenty male servants was considerable, so this costume tended to go with the job, being altered to fit new members of staff as required.

The wedding trousseau was a matter for much planning, discussion, and consultation with a number of shops and seamstresses. 'Wedding clothes' often called for a special visit to London to make purchases from shops called 'warehouses'. Sir Edward Knatchbull and Fanny Austen Knight visited London in August 1820 to order clothes for their October wedding. Numerous garments and accessories were purchased by each member of the new couple and represented a considerable expense for the families of both. In *Northanger Abbey* Eleanor Tilney's mother apparently had 'a very large fortune; and when she married, her father gave her twenty thousand pounds plus five hundred to buy wedding clothes. Mrs Hughes saw all the clothes after they came from the warehouse'. In 1791 Lady Bridges' household book records a disbursement of £800 for the wedding clothes of her three daughters. By comparison, the Reverend Austen's farm at Steventon cleared a profit of only £300 for the entire year of 1799.

The garments worn at weddings were as various then as now. The wedding of Miss Woodhouse and Mr Knightley (*Emma*) 'was very much like other weddings, where the parties have no taste for finery or parade', which Mrs Elton found rather dull: 'very little white satin, very few lace veils, a most pitiful business'. A detailed description of a wedding within the Austen family was given by Jane Austen's niece Caroline, whose half-sister Anna married Benjamin Lefroy on 8 November 1814. 'I and Anne Lefroy, nine and six years old, wore white frocks and had white ribband on a straw bonnet, which I suppose were new for the occasion.' The dress that Anna Austen wore for her wedding was later described by her own

*Fashions for girls were similar to those worn by their mothers. Adam Buck's portrait shows a demure young lady wearing a high-waisted muslin dress. The rather more unusual costume sported by the young gentleman in the Repository of the Arts, 1811, seems to reflect Chinese influence.*

daughter as being 'of a fine white muslin, and over it a soft silk shawl, white, shot with primrose, with embossed white satin flowers and the delicate yellow tints must have been most becoming to her bright brown hair, hazel eyes and sunny clear complexion.'

During the 1780s a fashion developed specifically for children. Girls began to be dressed in dainty, high-waisted muslin dresses, with perhaps a broad, coloured ribbon sash. The young Miss Bertrams in *Mansfield Park* could not help finding nine-year-old Fanny Price cheap when they perceived that 'she had but two sashes, and had never learnt French'. It was also during the 1780s that boys began to wear short, narrow-legged trousers or pantaloons, rather than breeches, which had previously been customary. Twenty years later, both these styles were adopted by adults. As with their mothers, white was the most popular colour for girls' dresses. In addition to muslin, nankeen and lightweight holland were popular for everyday wear, with silk reserved for best occasions. Spencers, pelisses and jackets with a cape were worn over girls' high-waisted dresses until about 1840, and from 1803 little girls began to wear pantaloons under their dresses. From about 1790 to 1830 the 'skeleton suit' was the most popular form of dress for young boys. It consisted of a jacket and trousers which buttoned together and were worn over a frilled shirt. From the age of about seven onwards boys wore a short jacket outside the trousers. The delightful drawings of Kate Greenaway (1846–1901) perfectly illustrate the styles of clothes worn by children of this period.

*Fashions on display* at an assembly room ball. *It was on such occasions that important social connections could be made, while young ladies and gentlemen, displaying all their finery, competed for advantageous and preferably agreeable marital partners:* The Cloakroom, Clifton Assembly Rooms, Bristol, 1817–18, by Rolinda Sharples. Inset: *Frontispiece to Wilson's* Companion to the Ballroom, *1816.*

One of the chief preoccupations of the English gentry, whether in the provinces or in London, was the pursuit of entertainment. The lively drawings of Thomas Rowlandson capture to perfection the carefree spirit of the age. Above: 'The Ball', from his series The Comforts of Bath, 1789. Opposite: A scene of music and dancing in London's Vauxhall Gardens, from The Microcosm of London, 1808.

# 5 · In Pursuit
of Entertainment

*

***London*** *was the Mecca for fashionable society. At private social engagements, held in elegant town-houses such as that shown* left *(inset:* 'Leaving a Party' *by Rowlandson), Jane Austen would have brushed shoulders with society's elite, while finding time to carry out 'commissions' in some of the world's most exquisite and well-stocked shops.* Above: *A shop-front in St James's St.*
Right: *Wedgwood and Byerley's shop on York St, St James, 1809.*

HE GENTRY had a great capacity for enjoying themselves, and always made time to be entertained and to provide hospitality and amusement for others. Furthermore, to be seen among elegant company in society's fashionable venues and resorts helped one to maintain a certain social standing. A season of up to four months in London, a month or six weeks in Bath or some other watering place, a month of travelling and six months at home, was not out of the ordinary, and would indeed be considered a very correct social calendar.

## London: Mecca of fashion

The tempo for entertaining was set in London, as the constant theme of fashionable elegance spread like a religion from the metropolis to more bucolic surroundings. London, with a population of nearly 700,000 in 1800, was not only the largest city in England, but had become the largest city in Europe as well. Three-quarters of the population of England and Wales lived in the countryside, but the aristocrats, nobles and gentry among them found their way to London for some portion of the year to experience the high-life and low-life of the bustling city, to attend theatres, concerts and exhibitions, to purchase imported goods from the marketplaces of the world – exquisitely displayed in the world's best shops – and to mix with the social elite. For this purpose many people kept 'a house in town' for the 'season', which was during the winter months. Others, such as Sir Thomas Bertram, MP (*Mansfield Park*), came while the government was in session, though Lady Bertram found it beyond her energies to accompany her husband; their daughter Maria entered her engagement to Mr Rushworth to 'assure her the house in town, which was now a prime object'.

One's address was a symbol of status. Maria obtained 'one of the best houses in Wimpole Street'; the John Dashwoods (*Sense and Sensibility*) were well situated in Harley Street; while the Bingleys (*Pride and Prejudice*) found equally upper-crust accommodation in Mr Hurst's house in Grosvenor Street. By constrast, the Gardiners, who were in trade, lived in Gracechurch Street, in the commercial district of London and within sight of Mr Gardiner's warehouse. Jane Austen's brother Henry and his wife Eliza were residents of London, and in 1801 Jane visited them at their home in fashionable Portman Square, where they lived 'quite in style'. The most stylish area was London's West End, formerly set out in streets and squares that were kept paved, clean and repaired, lighted at night and guarded by night-watchmen. The architecture was characterized by the mellow brick of the early Georgian period and the pattern-book regularity of Nash's Regency developments; all of these were in the somewhat verti-

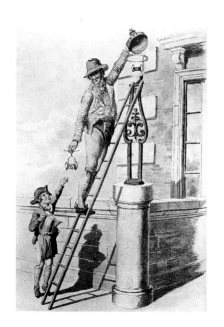

*Fashionable quarters of town, such as Portman Square (above right), home of Henry and Eliza Austen, were kept clean and well-lit (above left: a lamp-lighter of 1808).*

cal form of the three- or four-storey townhouse. A fashionable quarter was also growing up around Covent Garden, Piccadilly and Bloomsbury.

As the city grew, the various individual boroughs began to spread and connect with each other, though Chelsea, during Jane Austen's visits, was still a separate village. In 1809 the Henry Austens moved to Sloane Street, Knightsbridge, near the neighbourhood of Chelsea. The more pastoral atmosphere of this location probably appealed to Jane, though it was still within walking distance of the London shops. It was at the Sloane Street address, and during one of Jane's visits, that the socially aware Eliza Austen held a grand musical evening. This was the era when London's socially powerful chatelaines held drawing-room soirées, to which an invitation was an appointment to society's firmament of heaven. For Eliza's party the rooms were 'dressed up with flowers' and in the drawing room a 'glass for the Mantlepiece was lent' to complement the Austens' Empire-style furniture – tables like classical altars and hard, narrow sofas supported by swans and brooding lions. The windows were draped with yellow satin, powdered with gilt stars and slung from the beaks of brass eagles perched on the cornices. The floors were waxed and polished, and bare except for a few sheepskin rugs. In the air there was the faint scent of cedarwood and pot-pourri, and the perfume of the pink wax wall lights, as described by Helen Ashton in her book *Parson Austen's Daughter* (London, 1949). Henry had found a merchant in the city who provided the occasion with smuggled French champagne, while their further sustenance was prepared by the Austens' French cook, Madame Bigeon, and consisted of soups and sauces, hot lobster, oyster pâtés and cold chicken aspic, followed by ices and little heart-shaped French cakes soaked in rum. Eliza wore a high-waisted gown of pale yellow, and cameo jewelry, with a scarf of gilt tissue wrapped twice around her arms; her hair was dressed in countless silver-grey curls.

**The theatre** *was a popular source of entertainment.* Opposite: *The Theatre Royal, opened in Bath in 1805. It was here, in this elegant gold and crimson interior, now restored to its former splendour, that Charles Musgrove secured a box for a Saturday evening performance (*Persuasion*). Such famous thespians as Mrs Siddons (*inset*) and Edmund Kean enthralled audiences of the period in Bath and London; Jane saw Kean as Shylock (*left*) at Drury Lane in 1814. A painting by Zoffany of David Garrick in* The Farmer's Return, *from Stoneleigh Abbey (*above*).*

The stifling atmosphere of some of London's private parties is depicted in *Sense and Sensibility*; Elinor and Marianne, accompanying Lady Middleton, 'entered a room splendidly lit up, quite full of company, and insufferably hot. When they had paid their tribute of politeness by curtseying to the lady of the house, they were permitted to mingle with the crowd, and take their share of the heat and inconvenience, to which their arrival must necessarily add. After some time in saying little, and doing less, Lady Middleton sat down to casino . . . .'

London hummed with the traffic of goods and traders. The steady cry of street pedlars found its merchant counterpart in the foppish manner of West End shopkeepers. In 1800 there were 150 shops in Oxford Street alone, and Jane always made time to treat herself in the city shops and to make purchases on behalf of friends and relatives in the country. She mentions buying muslin and trimmings at Grafton's the drapers, as well as purchases of gloves, stockings, caps, bonnets, china from Wedgwood's shop and tea from Twinings. In Gray's the jewelers on Sackville Street Mr John Dashwood, encountering his half-sister, excuses himself for not calling on her, as 'one always has so much to do on first coming to town, I am come here to bespeak Fanny a seal'. Also in the shop is a boorish dandy choosing a toothpick case adorned with ivory, gold and pearls. In *Emma* Mr Elton takes Harriet's picture to London to be framed in Bond Street, and Frank Churchill goes there to have his hair cut – though this is only an excuse contrived to conceal his true purpose, which is to purchase a piano for the woman he loves.

For cultural amusement London had several theatres, concert halls and galleries. In her letters Jane Austen mentions visits with her nieces and nephews to the Lyceum Theatre and to Covent Garden, where 'the Clandestine Marriage was the most respectable of the performances, the rest were sing-song & trumpery, but did very well for Lizzy & Marianne, who were indeed delighted; – but *I* wanted better acting' (to Francis Austen, 25 Setember 1813). Theatrical performances usually lasted five or six hours and consisted of two dissimilar plays with opera, farce or ballet preceding and following the main performance. In a letter of 1814 Jane wrote of an evening of Italian opera: 'I was very tired of Artaxerxes, highly amused with the Farce, & in an inferior way with the Pantomime that followed.'

London theatre-goers were not always easy to play to, as suggested in an article in the *London Chronicle* of 1 November 1811, describing an opening night at the Lyceum Theatre: 'last night was produced here for the first time a comedy in five acts called "The Kiss" . . . – the performance was frequently interrupted by loud indications of dislike, which often rendered what was passing on the stage inaudible; and at the dropping of the curtain, the clamour of dissatisfaction appeared to outroar the breath of praise'. But it was in Georgian London that the great Thespians David Garrick, John Kemble, Mrs Siddons and Edmund Kean graced the stage. In 1811 Jane Austen was disappointed of seeing Mrs Siddons: 'She *did* act on Monday, but as Henry was told by the Boxkeeper that he did not think

*Attending an exhibition of watercolours was among the delights of London enjoyed by Jane Austen in 1811, though it was mainly people – whether the subjects of portraits, or other visitors to the exhibitions – who tended to interest her most.*

she would, the places, & all thought of it, were given up. I should particularly have liked seeing her in *Constance*, & could swear at her with little effort for disappointing me.' In 1814, however, she did manage to see the tragedian Edmund Kean in *The Merchant of Venice* at Drury Lane, 'but so great is the rage for seeing Kean that only a third and fourth row could be got'. Three days later she reported, 'We were quite satisfied with Kean. I cannot imagine better acting'.

A stage performance of another kind was a horse-riding display held at Astley's Royal Amphitheatre and attended by Harriet Smith and the John Knightleys in *Emma*; Jane Austen also enjoyed a performance at Astley's in 1796. This type of entertainment was fairly similar to the modern-day circus.

During this era of the great English artists Constable and Turner, Jane Austen gives us disappointingly few details of her visits to exhibitions. In 1811 she mentions the Liverpool Museum and the British Gallery: 'I had some amusement at each, tho' my preference for Men & Women, always inclines me to attend more to the company than the sight'; and a week later she wrote, 'Henry has been to the Watercolour Exhibition, which open'd on Monday, & is to meet us there again some morn$^g$.' At the exhibitions of portrait artists which she attended in 1813, she playfully searched among the paintings for the countenances of her characters:

**Bath** *was, next to London, the most fashionable venue for the cream of society.*
Left: *One of the beauties of Bath, Pulteney Bridge, designed by Robert Adam and completed in 1774. It remains as it was during Jane Austen's visits and residence in the city.* Above: *Landsdowne Crescent, surmounting Lansdowne Hill, described in the Bath guide of 1800 as 'one of the most ... happily situated hills in the west of England, and famous for the number of sheep fattened by its herbage'.*
Right: *The Colonnades.*

Henry & I went to the Exhibition in Spring Gardens [Society of Painters Exhibition]. It is not thought a good collection, but I was very well pleased – particularly (pray tell Fanny) with a small portrait of Mrs. Bingley, excessively like her. I went in hopes of seeing one of her Sister, but there was no Mrs. Darcy; – perhaps however, I may find her in the Great Exhibition [that of the British Academy in Somerset Place] which we shall go to, if we have time; – I have no chance of her in the collection of Sir Joshua Reynolds's Paintings which is now shewing in Pall Mall, & which we are also to visit. [The British Institution was showing '130 of his performances'.] Mrs. Bingley's is exactly herself, size, shaped face, features & sweetness; there never was a greater likeness. She is dressed in a white gown, with green ornaments, which convinces me of what I had always supposed, that green was a favourite colour with her. I daresay Mrs. D. will be in Yellow.

Of her visits to London, Jane Austen mentions drives through the city streets: in 1813, 'the Driving about, the Carriage being open, was very pleasant. – I liked my solitary elegance very much, & was ready to laugh all the time, at my being where I was. – I could not but feel that I had naturally small right to be parading about London in a Barouche.' She also refers to walks in Kensington Gardens. For the entertainment of the populace there were various tea gardens, 'frequented by the middling classes on Sunday especially', and the Vauxhall pleasure gardens, which continued with undiminished popularity until 1859. There, under a thousand lamps, one could enjoy vocal concerts, tight-rope artists, jugglers and equestrian feats followed by a burst of fireworks. Equestrianism was popularized by well-mounted men and women seen riding in the parks and high roads. The indelicate amusement of pugilism was patronized by gentlemen and the lower ranks alike, as was animal-baiting, though the latter diminished in popularity as the nineteenth century began to adopt Victorian values.

A famous place of entertainment closely associated with London's most elite society was Almack's. A private club founded in 1764, it had by the turn of the century become an assembly for dancing, gambling and gossip, run by a female oligarchy whose despotic selectness had once turned away the Duke of Wellington from its portals. 'This is selection with a vengeance; the very quintessence of aristocracy', said a writer in the *New Monthly Magazine* in 1814; 'Three fourths of the nobility knock in vain for admission.' In 1796 Eliza, then the Comtesse de Feuillide, enjoyed the rarefied company of Almack's until five in the morning.

Gentlemen's clubs, most notably Brook's, Boodle's and White's, were headquarters for gambling. But these and other West End clubs were eventually superseded in their worship of the goddess of chance by Waiter's, which became the greatest gambling club in London. Started in 1805, it supposedly found existence through a whim of the Prince, who enquired of some members of White's and Brook's who were dining with

*The Crimson Drawing Room of the Prince Regent's residence, Carlton House, London, which Jane visited in 1815.* Right: *The handsomely bound edition of* Emma *presented to the Regent.*

him, what sort of fare they received at their clubs? Sir Thomas Stepney replied that the food was horribly monotonous, whereupon the Prince rang for a waiter, and on his appearance, asked him to take a house and organize a club. No. 81 Piccadilly was secured, and Waiter's club began.

It was in 1812 that the word 'slum' entered the English language, and certainly Jane Austen could not have been unaware of the squalor and perilous existence that were the lot of many of London's inhabitants. In the novels one is given a foreboding of the evils that exist in the city. In *Sense and Sensibility* Colonel Brandon's childhood friend Eliza, left destitute and friendless in London, changes from 'a lovely blooming healthful girl' to a 'melancholy and sickly figure'. But for the most part Jane Austen took a balanced view and, while being aware of the misery that clung about London, enjoyed the city's excitement, society and amusements.

During her last visit to London in 1815, she had the honour of being shown the Prince Regent's residence, Carlton House. The house had been remodelled at great expense by Henry Holland. The style was predominantly French, and dazzled with silver and gold decoration. Her host, the Prince's domestic chaplain, the haughty Reverend James Stanier Clarke, showed Jane the fan-vaulted conservatory, the round second drawing room, dining hall and forty-foot library, among other rooms, and while showing her these apartments he intimated that the dedication of her new book to the Prince would not be found unacceptable. Subsequent to this visit, *Emma* was 'most respectfully dedicated' to His Royal Highness the Prince Regent 'by His Royal Highness's dutiful and obedient humble servant The Author'.

# Bath: a season of pleasurable pursuits

Bath is perhaps the most perfect example of town planning: a classical city with a uniformity of materials and design contrived to make individual houses appear as a single great mansion. Primarily the inspiration of its most celebrated architect, John Wood (1704–54), it is a city of hills, like Rome, and – imitating ancient Rome – it was criss-crossed with paved, manicured streets, interspersed with circular arrangements of buildings and spaces for promenading. Elegant visitors were whisked up and down the city's seven hills in sedan chairs by formidable Irish bearers. Assembly rooms, theatres and pleasure gardens were created for socializing, and a correct, civilized routine was ordered for the conduct of guests and inhabitants. The latter was instituted by Richard 'Beau' Nash, who came to Bath in 1705 and became the city's official Master of Ceremonies; a polished though inveterate gambler and womanizer, Nash was aptly suited for cleaning up Bath's increasingly robust and risqué image. His dictums set the standard, and just as Bath's architecture influenced the townscapes of England, so did its rules of etiquette influence the manners of the entire nation throughout the Georgian era.

During the first quarter of the eighteenth century, Bath became established as a resort for health and pleasure, but it was not until the second half of the century that the numbers of wealthy and fashionable visitors were so great as to inspire entrepreneurs to develop comfortable accommodation and buildings for entertainment and leisure. By 1800 an official guide book reads: 'The city of Bath has so considerably increased in size and the number of its inhabitants, that it has become one of the *most agreeable* as well as *most polite* places in the Kingdom; owing chiefly to the elegant neatness of its buildings, and the accommodations for strangers, which are superior to those of any city in Europe.'

It was to the sedate Bath that Jane Austen made several visits; her first appears to have been in November 1797 as the guest of her aunt and uncle, the Leigh-Perrots, who were winter residents of the city throughout Jane's lifetime. In 1799 Jane and her mother accompanied her brother Edward to Bath along with Edward's wife Elizabeth and their two eldest children, Fanny and Edward. The family took lodgings at 13 Queen's Square, and the *Bath Chronicle* for Thursday 23 May 1799 included among the new arrivals for that week 'Mr. and Mrs. E. Austin'; as the heir to a great estate, Edward was worthy of the newspaper's notice. In addition to weekly announcements in the paper, worthies were invited to leave their names and Bath address in the books designed for that purpose located in the pump rooms. Indeed, in 1787 it was decreed

> That ladies and gentlemen coming to town, give orders that their names and places of abode be entered in any of the Pump-Room books; and the Master of Ceremonies thus publickly requests the favour of such Ladies and Gentlemen, to whom he has not the honour of being personally known, to offer him some favourable occasion of

*The orderly and elegant city of Bath as Jane would have known it, set against its backdrop of hills:* The Axford and Paragon Buildings, *1806, J.G. Nattes.*

being presented to them, that he may be enabled to shew that attention, which is not more his duty than his inclination to observe.

It is through examining 'the book' that Catherine Morland learns the address in Milsom Street where the Tilneys have their lodgings. The signatory to the notice of 1787 was James King, Master of Ceremonies at the Lower Rooms, and in *Northanger Abbey* it is a 'Mr King' who introduces Henry Tilney to Catherine, at her first dance at the Lower Rooms.

A good address got one off on the right footing among the resort's compact society, and as it was such public information, the importance of choosing lodgings in a correct neighbourhood could not be overlooked. The wealthy would take an entire house, those with less to spend, half a house or just a floor. The internal arrangements and furnishings of accommodation varied according to the requirements of the leaseholders, so that some were sumptuously appointed to suit an individual taste, while others, intended for casual letting, provided only the basics. Tenants, whatever their stature, were expected to bring their own linen and plate, as well as their own servants. In a letter to her sister, Jane Austen described the Queen's Square accommodation:

> We are exceedingly pleased with the house; the rooms are quite as large as we expected. Mrs. Bromley is a fat woman in mourning, and a little black kitten runs about the staircase. Elizabeth has the apartment within the drawing-room; ... it is settled for us to be above, where we have two very nice-sized rooms.... I like our situation very much; ... and the prospect from the drawing room window, at which I now write, is rather picturesque, as it commands a perspective view of the left side of Brock Street, broken by three Lombardy poplars in the garden of the last house in Queen's Parade. (17 May 1799)

In *Persuasion* Lady Dalrymple had taken a house, for three months, in

Laura Place, and would be living in style, and Sir Walter Elliot was ready to admit Colonel Wallis as an acquaintance because his wife was said to be very pretty and because he was 'living in a very good style in Marlborough Buildings'. Marlborough Buildings overlooked the Royal Crescent, another premier address. For his own comfort, 'Sir Walter had taken a very good house in Camden-Place [later known as Camden Crescent], a lofty dignified situation such as becomes a man of consequence; and both he and [his daughter] Elizabeth were settled there, much to their satisfaction.... Their house was undoubtedly the best in Camden-Place. Everybody was wanting to visit them.'

Once the visitor was settled into a house or lodgings and registered in the 'book', the delights of Bath awaited. The Bath guide of 1802 explained that:

> There are two dress balls every week, viz. on Monday at the New Rooms [the Upper Rooms], and Friday at the Lower Rooms.... There are also two Fancy Balls every week, viz. at the Lower Rooms on Tuesday, and at the New Rooms on Thursday [and] Nine subscription concerts, and three choral nights, in the winter at the New Rooms, on Wednesday, under the direction of Mr Rauzzini.

For ladies and gentlemen with money and at leisure to spend it, Bath offered an enormous array of fashionable shops, second only to London. The three principal shopping streets mentioned in the novels are Bond Street, Milsom Street and Bath Street. Admiral Croft was tempted by the display in the window of a print shop, and Captain Harville's 'business' was to choose a frame for the miniature of Captain Benwick, while Henrietta Musgrove came to Bath to 'buy wedding-clothes for herself and her sister' (*Persuasion*). Elegant gowns, trimmings and exquisite accessories were available in abundance. Mrs Allen in *Northanger Abbey* thought Bath a charming town: 'There are so many good shops here. – We are sadly off in the country; not but what we have very good shops in Salisbury, but it is so far to go; eight miles is a long way.... Now here one can step out of doors and get a thing in five minutes.' When she and Catherine Morland arrive in Bath from Wiltshire, before engaging in any public or social activities they spend 'three or four days ... in learning what was mostly worn, and buying clothes of the latest fashion.'

Another of the glories of shopping in Bath were the food markets. For 150 years Bath had been a centre for gourmets in England. Regional specialities such as cheddar cheese, sole, turbot and sturgeon from the Severn estuary, and Welsh mountain mutton were sought by cooks, ladies, ladies' maids and gentlemen, bargaining side by side in the city's food markets. Foodstuffs were also purchased in the city and loaded into flying coaches for despatch throughout England. Local physician Doctor Oliver invented a plain biscuit to counteract the residents' obsession with rich food. The bun was also invented in Bath under the name of Sally Lunn, its first maker, who kept a pastrycook's shop in the city. In *Northanger Abbey* parties of ladies crossed Cheap Street 'in quest of millinery or pastry', and in 1799 Jane wrote to Cassandra of her brother Edward, 'I trust the bustle of sending for tea, coffee, and sugar, & c., and going out to taste a cheese himself, will do him good.'

Whatever the fashionable amusements that wooed visitors to Bath throughout the eighteenth century, they initially came seeking the waters as a cure for various ailments. Jane's brother Edward came in 1797 to remedy his ailing health, and her uncle Mr Leigh-Perrot took a regular dose of mineral water from the pump rooms. 'It will be too tedious at present', said the Bath guide of 1800, 'to enumerate all the diseases curable by Bath Water, internally taken or externally used. Many people have come to Bath, tired with taking medicines (at home) to no manner of purpose at all; they have drank the Bath water with abundance of delight and pleasure, and by the help of a little physic have recovered to admiration'. Those who had more serious afflictions, such as Mrs Smith in *Persuasion*, who suffered from rheumatic fever, not only drank the water but also bathed in it. Mr Allen (*Northanger Abbey*) 'was ordered to Bath for the benefit of a gouty constitution', but happily for those who accompanied him, Mrs Allen and Catherine Morland, the city also offered interesting diversions for the healthy.

There were three pumps in the city which collected waters from the thermal springs through faults in the rock below the surface of Bath. The favoured pump was King's Bath, closest to the abbey, with a fine pump room that was built in 1706 and enlarged in the last decade of the eighteenth century. According to the 1800 Bath guide, 'the nobility and gentry assemble in it every morning, between the hours of seven and ten, to drink the water; for whose entertainment a good band of musick attends during the season'. 'In the morning', said the same guide, 'the rendez-vous is at the Pump-Room; – from that time till noon in walking on the Parades, or in the different quarters of the town; thence to the Pump-Room again, and after a fresh stroll, to dinner'. One o'clock is the hour Catherine and Isabella 'meet by appointment' in the pump rooms and it is also the hour that Catherine goes there to search for her new friend, Eleanor Tilney, since 'in the Pump Room one so newly arrived must be met with' (*Northanger Abbey*).

After a morning spent shopping or in the pump room examining the new arrivals to the city, followed by a promenade among the fashionable squares and crescents, part of the day would probably be spent paying and receiving morning calls. (Morning was then the period from waking until dinner, which was served at any time between four and half-past six.) As with most resort towns, friendships were quickly formed. In Bath new acquaintances were the means to an introduction to other fashionable visitors, so as to be placed among the select society, although back in London these 'friendships' were quickly forgotten. Another of the day's diversions might involve a carriage ride or a walk among the city's hills and surrounding countryside. Catherine Morland looks for Henry Tilney 'among the walkers, the horsemen or the curricle-drivers of the morning' (*Northanger Abbey*), and is taken for a drive, as was Jane Austen: 'There is

now something like an engagement between us & the Phaeton, which to confess my frailty I have a great desire to go out in', she wrote to her sister in 1801; her 'gentleman coachman' was a Mr Evelyn, a friend of her brother Edward. The following day she wrote, 'I am just returned from my airing in the very bewitching Phaeton & four, for which I was prepared by a note from M^r E. soon after breakfast: We went to the top of Kingsdown & had a very pleasant drive.'

Jane Austen also enjoyed frequent country walks during her stays in Bath. In *Northanger Abbey*, 'Miss Tilney, to whom all the commonly-frequented environs were familiar', spoke of country walks in terms that made Catherine Morland 'all eagerness to know them too'. The walk that resulted from this dialogue was to Beechen Cliff, 'that noble hill, whose beautiful verdure and hanging coppice render it so striking an object from almost every opening in Bath.' Social walking of a less energetic kind was performed, especially on Sundays, in the city itself, the most fashionable location being the 'Crescent fields', the green slopes in front of the Royal Crescent.

a fine Sunday in Bath empties every house of its inhabitants, and all the world appears on such an occasion to walk about and tell their acquaintance what a charming day it is. As soon as divine service was over, the Thorpes and Allens eagerly joined each other; and after staying long enough in the pump-room to discover that the crowd was insupportable, and that there was not a genteel face to be seen, which everybody discovers every Sunday throughout the season, they hastened away to the Crescent, to breathe the fresh air of better company. (*Northanger Abbey*)

Jane Austen also mentions walking in the Crescent in 1801: 'We did not walk long in the Crescent yesterday, it was hot & not crouded enough; so we went into the field'. It was not only on Sundays that people might reasonably hope to meet their friends promenading on the broad pavements of the Crescent. Mrs Allen and Mrs Thorpe (*Northanger Abbey*) meet in the pump room and 'agree to take a turn in the Crescent'; there they encounter Mrs Hughes and the young Tilneys, with whom they 'walked along the Crescent together for half an hour'.

Alternatively, amusement could be obtained by becoming a subscriber to a library. Generally the pastime of women, this entailed an annual membership that cost the likes of Isabella Thorpe or Catherine Morland (*Northanger Abbey*) up to one guinea, with an additional fee of one penny for each volume borrowed. The library was a feature of most resorts during this period. At the time of Jane's visit to Bath in 1801, the *Bath Journal* advertised a selection of new books, including some rather titillating Gothic titles: *Castle of St Donats*, *Fugitive of the Forest*, *The Nocturnal Visit*, *Children of the Abbey*, *Monk of the Grotto* and *Emily of Lucerne*.

Dancing, listening to music and going to the theatre were the main occupations of the evening, with the addition of card-playing, available in the ante-room adjoining the main ballroom of most assembly rooms, for those who, like Mr Allen, preferred not to dance. At the Lower Rooms, the Master of Ceremonies introduces Catherine Morland to Henry Tilney. The couple dance, and afterwards take tea and become better acquainted as Mr Tilney gently interrogates his companion:

'I have not yet asked you how long you have been in Bath; whether you were ever here before; whether you have been at the Upper Rooms, the theatre, and the concert; and how you like the place altogether. I have been very negligent – but are you now at leisure to satisfy me in these particulars? If you are I will begin directly. . . . Were you never here before, madam?'

'Never, sir.'

'Indeed! Have you yet honoured the Upper Rooms?'

'Yes, sir, I was there last Monday.'

'Have you been to the theatre?'

'Yes, sir, I was at the play on Tuesday.'

'To the concert?'

'Yes, sir, on Wednesday.'

'And are you altogether pleased with Bath?'

'Yes – I like it very well.'

Thus was a week's evening entertainment arranged. The pattern set earlier in the century by 'Beau' Nash, whose regulations on conduct extended to arrangements for public assemblies, was still being followed in the 1790s during the writing of *Northanger Abbey*: dancing was to 'begin as soon as possible after six o'clock, and finish *precisely* at eleven, even in the middle of a dance'. Nash, a professional gambler, also encouraged what was to become another tradition – high play organized in elegant private gambling saloons.

The city had two 'sets' of assembly rooms, the Lower Rooms and the Upper Rooms. The Lower Rooms date from 1708, with additions in 1720 and 1749, and were well situated for that time, being near the bowling green, parades and river walks. 'There is a publick breakfast or agreeable morning promenade every Wednesday, at the Lower Rooms, during the season', stated a guide. By 1806 Mr King had been succeeded as Master of Ceremonies there by Mr Le Bas, who is mentioned in a letter from Mrs Austen: 'Mr. Le Bas's Ball on Friday at the Lower Rooms will probably be but a thin one'.

As the town expanded up the northern slopes, convenience required the building of the Upper Rooms between 1769 and 1771. There was considerable rivalry between the two sets of rooms, yet by offering attractions on alternate evenings, both managed to stay in business well into the nineteenth century, when the Lower Rooms eventually fell into disuse. In 1801 Jane Austen wrote a description of an assembly she attended at the Upper Rooms:

> In the evening I hope you honoured my Toilette & Ball with a thought; I dressed myself as well as I could, & had all my finery much admired at home. By nine o'clock my Uncle, Aunt & I entered the rooms & linked Miss Winstone on to us. – Before tea, it was rather a dull affair; but then the before tea did not last long, for there was only one dance, danced by four couple. – Think of four couple, surrounded by about an hundred people, dancing in the upper Rooms at Bath! – After tea we *cheered up*; the breaking up of private parties sent some scores more to the Ball, & tho' it was shockingly & inhumanly thin for

this place, there were people enough I suppose to have made five or six very pretty Basingstoke assemblies.

The shortage of people may have been because the season was coming to an end. In 1808 Mrs Austen wrote of the Upper Rooms, 'ball on Monday was not a very *full* one, not more than *a thousand*'.

The theatre that Catherine Morland attended was the old theatre on Orchard Street near the abbey. It was built in 1750, and in 1768 was granted a royal patent, becoming the first provincial playhouse entitled to call itself 'Theatre Royal'. The auditorium was rectangular and lined with boxes, which contained seats bookable in advance. In 1799 Jane Austen saw Charles Dibden's *The Birthday* and *Bluebeard*, for it was the custom for two plays to be performed each evening. *Lovers' Vows*, the play so important to the plot of *Mansfield Park*, is estimated to have been performed there on six separate engagements. The last performance at the Orchard Street house was *Venice Preserv'd*, given on 13 July 1805. In October of that year a new theatre opened in Bath with the performance of Shakespeare's *Richard III*; the afterpiece on the playbill was *Poor Soldier*. It was at this new theatre, with its elegant gold and crimson interior, that Charles Musgrove (*Persuasion*) secured a box to seat nine for a Saturday evening performance. That great Shakespearian enchantress Mrs Siddons and her brother John Kemble regularly played to Bath audiences of this period.

Concerts performed during the season generally included choral works and soloists, a tradition established by Thomas Linley, who was the Director of Concerts in Bath from the mid-1750s to the 1770s. Two of his daughters, Elizabeth and Mary, were notable sopranos who had appeared at the Three Choirs Festival in London as well as in Bath. (Elizabeth later married the playwright Richard Brinsley Sheridan.) In *Persuasion* Anne Elliot attended 'a concert for the benefit of a person patronised by Lady Dalrymple'; Anne 'was quite impatient for the concert evening', and 'Captain Wentworth was very fond of music'. Jane Austen did not share her characters' fondness for concerts. In a letter from Queen's Square in 1799, she wrote: 'There is to be a grand gala on tuesday evening in Sydney Gardens; – a Concert, with Illuminations & fireworks; – to the latter Eliz: & I look forward with pleasure, & even the Concert will have more than it's usual charm with me, as the gardens are large enough for me to get pretty well beyond the reach of its sound.' During the day Sydney Gardens was the venue for public breakfasts, which Jane mentions attending in 1799. These were held on Mondays and Thursdays and were well attended throughout the season. Tea, cakes and rolls were served to the accompaniment of French horns and clarinets. When the Austens were later considering a home near Sydney Gardens as their residence Jane wrote: 'It would be very pleasant to be near Sidney Gardens! – we might go into the Labyrinth every day.' Surrounding the gardens was a 'Ride for the accommodation of ladies and gentlemen on horseback'. Indeed, riding became a popular form of equestrian promenading among the leisured visitors to Bath.

*In 1801 the Austens moved to 4 Sydney Place, across the road from Sydney Gardens – shown here in an engraving by J.G. Nattes of 1806.*

Bath at the beginning of the nineteenth century was in the decline of its fashion. Public social gatherings were replaced by private parties, and a greater share of visitors to the city were the infirm, the elderly, retired, or widows and widowers among the gentry and the middle classes. Elderly but elegant gentlewomen continued to come to Bath for treatment. Lady Bridges went to Bath in 1813, where she was joined by her son-in-law Edward and her grand-daughter Fanny Austen Knight. Fanny attended two balls at the Upper and Lower Rooms, respectively, which she later described to her friend Miss Chapman as being 'very stupid'. Malvern in Worcestershire and Cheltenham in Gloucestershire vied with Bath in attracting the valetudinarian, while the Kent spa Tunbridge Wells remained fashionable for retiring Londoners well into the nineteenth century.

## *By the sea*

Seaside resorts came into vogue in 1789 when George III paid a visit to Weymouth. These resorts gradually began to replace inland spas as holiday retreats, and like the spas, their initial attraction was as a tonic to good health. In the eighteenth century sea water was thought to be a remedy for all kinds of complaints, the benefits being derived both from bathing in it and drinking it. As the coastal resorts gained in favour, social activities were added to the medicinal attractions.

The Austen family made several excursions to the south coast of England during their residence in Bath: to Sidmouth, Teignmouth and Dawlish in Devon, Ramsgate in Kent (later frequented by the young Princess Victoria), and Lyme Regis in Dorset. In *Persuasion* Jane Austen describes Lyme Regis, with 'the principal street almost hurrying into the water', and 'the pleasant little bay, which in the season is animated with bathing-machines and company'. The bathing-machine was a wooden hut on wheels drawn by horses, in which the occupant changed into garments suitable for bathing; the whole structure was then dragged by the horses into the water, and the bather was submerged. This latter stage of the operation was assisted by large individuals, often women, known as 'dippers'. Although the scenery of Lyme appealed to Jane, she found their lodgings there somewhat makeshift and inconvenient. Her niece Miss Lefroy later described the Austens' accommodation as having 'two ground floors, one in its proper place and the other at the top of the house containing the bedrooms and back door, which latter opened on to the green hill behind'. The sitting room is said to have been pretty, and by climbing steps to one of the garden seats one could command a view of the sea – a feature that may have accounted for the name of the lodging house, 'Wings'.

The Knight family also enjoyed visits to the sea coast, and in 1806 Fanny Austen Knight recalled an outing to Deal, on the Kent coast, in a letter to Miss Chapman:

> We eat, walked on the Beach, & at ½ past 1, a Boat from the Princess of Orange (whose Captain, is a friend of Uncle Bridge's) arrived to take us on board, with Capt.ⁿ [Hor-] himself. She lay about 2 miles

*Bathing-machines could always be seen scattered along the beaches and in the shallow waters of seaside resorts. These vehicles allowed modest bathers of the upper classes to make their entry into the health-giving water while retaining a high degree of privacy.*

*Many resorts on the south coast of England became popular as holiday retreats. Lyme Regis in Dorset (*right*) was a particular favourite with the Austen family.* Left: *Bathing place evening dress, from La Belle Assemblée, 1810.*

out, but we took a pleasant sail of 4 or 5 miles round & were none of us at all sick. It was very good fun to hear the Capt.[n] himself give the orders to the sailors, I never can help laughing at the odd sea terms '*Jib the mizzens*'; *Up the foresheet*; *Down the Main Sail, Port the Helm, we're going starboard side, go to Leeward*; etc etc then we enjoyed being whirled up in a chair, & I never was more amused than in going over the ship. Only think how curious to see a Blacksmith's forge, a kitchen fireplace larger than many of ours, comfortable little apartments with women working in them all in a ship! The Princess of Orange is a very fine ship [. . .]; the Carpenter very much amused us for when he shewed us his Cabins, there was a woman sitting at work, & he said 'Ladies this is my Cabin, & this is my *Spouse*' & indeed he had reason to be proud of her, for she seemed neater and cleaner than the generality of women. We returned to Deal to dinner & to Goodnestone in the evening to an excellent supper of muttons broth, & never was bed more acceptable to any of the party I believe.

By 1815 the Kent coast had become so popular that there were steamboats on the Thames taking holidaymakers to Margate, Ramsgate and Broadstairs.

Those at the apex of London's social pyramid followed the Prince Regent to Brighton; he first distinguished the Sussex coastal resort with royal visits in 1784. When England declared war on France in 1793, it became necessary to prepare for the defence of the vulnerable south coast, and by the summer of that year ten thousand troops were encamped around Brighton, including the Tenth Light Dragoons, of which the Prince was colonel-in-chief. For his comfort he was provided with a grand

tent, 'the most elegant ever made in England'. The garrison remained stationed at Brighton for more than twelve years, and for Lydia Bennet (*Pride and Prejudice*) the soldiers were a welcome addition to the resort's other amusements; she imagined 'with the creative eye of fancy, the streets of that gay bathing place covered with officers', and had visions of a glorious camp dazzling with scarlet and of 'herself seated beneath a tent, tenderly flirting with at least six officers at once.'

In addition to sea cures and select socializing, Brighton also offered more profligate entertainments, such as horse-racing, prize-fighting and a certain amount of debauchery. It was not only the Prince's enthusiasm for the turf that attracted the upper classes to race meetings. The sport had been patronized by nobles and gentry since the Oaks were initiated by the Earl of Derby in 1779, and the Derby itself in 1780. That some members of the Austen family took pleasure in this pastime is indicated in a letter of Fanny Austen Knight to Miss Chapman:

> Were you at any part of the Races? I shall be vexed to death if you were at the course, any day, particularly Wednesday, which day we were there, that is to say Capt$^n$ & Mrs H$^y$ Austen, the three boys, & I to meet the Goodnestone Party, which was very pleasant. Have you heard who were the Belles of the Races? They *say* Aunt Harriot & Lucy Foote were – (Godmersham Park, August 1806)

In *Mansfield Park* Tom Bertram has a weakness for the races, and when Mary Crawford sets her sights on this heir to the Mansfield estate, she decides 'to interest herself a little about the horse which he had run at the B-Races'.

*A lively scene at the races that would have been relished by Tom Bertram (*Breaking the Course, *1803, by William Fellows).*

These Races were to call him away not long after their acquaintance began; and as it appeared that the family did not, from his usual goings on, expect him back again for many weeks, it would bring his passion to an early proof. Much was said on his side to induce her to attend the Races, and schemes were made for a large party of them, with all the eagerness of inclination, but it would only do to be talked of.

Tom was later to meet with an accident at the Newmarket Races.

## The age of travel

Jane Austen's lifetime coincided with the great age of coach travel. Roads were steadily improved as the gentry travelled from their country seats to London for the season and on to Bath, the seaside resorts and other watering places. Travel for its own sake had also become fashionable as an enjoyable means of broadening one's aesthetic experience, by journeying to the farther reaches of England and Scotland in quest of a 'picturesque' landscape.

Like the celebrated travel writer William Gilpin, Elizabeth Bennet and the Gardiners planned to travel north:

'We have not quite determined how far it shall carry us,' said Mrs Gardiner, 'but perhaps to the Lakes'.

No scheme could have been more agreeable to Elizabeth, and her acceptance of the invitation was most ready and grateful. 'My dear, dear aunt,' she rapturously cried, 'what delight! what felicity! You give me fresh life and vigour. *Adieu* to disappointment and spleen. What are men to rocks and mountains? Oh! what hours of transport shall we spend! And when we *do* return, it shall not be like other travellers, without being able to give one accurate idea of any thing. We *will* know where we have gone – we *will* recollect what we have seen. Lakes, mountains and rivers shall not be jumbled together in our imaginations; nor, when we attempt to describe any particular scene, will we begin quarrelling about its relative situation. Let *our* first effusions be less insupportable than those of the generality of travellers.'

As it happened, 'they were obliged to give up the Lakes, and substitute a more contracted tour'; their journey took them no farther northward than Derbyshire, where they visited Chatsworth and Mr Darcy's country house, Pemberley. Visits to the country seats of the wealthy were becoming popular outings for both the English and foreigners. Housekeepers of the great houses were well skilled in guiding visitors through their establishments, pointing out the portraits of noble ancestors, their master's fine taste in the choice of furnishings, the elegance of the rooms and the splendour of the vistas. Outside, a retinue of groundsmen and gardeners would appear to explain the laying out of the park or the technology of the forcing gardens, all of them hat in hand with the other hand extended in expectation of some monetary reward for their exertions.

Day trips to visit the ruins of abbeys or castles were also popular. During her week's stay at Stoneleigh Abbey, Warwickshire, in 1806 Jane Austen made visits to Warwick Castle and to Kenilworth Castle. These outings probably included some 'cold collation', as did the Box Hill excursion in *Emma*. The seven-mile journey to Box Hill is travelled in two carriages and in expectation of enjoyment, and upon first arriving, everybody expresses a burst of admiration. Gilpin's description of Box Hill contributed to the fame of this Surrey beauty spot: 'This hill from its downy back and precipitous sides, exhibits great variety of pleasing views into the lower parts of Surrey; and the higher parts of the neighbouring counties'. But for the travellers from Highbury, the vistas and hillside picnic fail to raise the spirits of the company.

The keeping of carriages and horses was an outward sign of material wealth during Georgian times. The sleekness of the equipage and the

*Repton's depiction of a picnic at Longleat, 1816, is reminiscent of the Box Hill excursion in* Emma. *Trips to natural beauty spots and famous country houses were very much in vogue, and were facilitated by the greater ease of travel that resulted from improved roads.*

*The keeping of carriages was an outward sign of one's wealth and position.* Left: *The Prince Regent driving a curricle to Brighton.* Opposite: *An elegant chariot from* The Sporting Magazine, *rather like the elaborately decorated model ordered by Chandos Leigh, and a plain coach of 1796 – a more practical vehicle.*

quality of the livery worn by the attendants were strong testaments to the owner's importance. The connection between one's position and means of travel is variously indicated in the novels: the Tilneys of *Northanger Abbey* travel in a 'fashionable chaise-and-four-postilions handsomely liveried . . . numerous out-riders properly mounted'; in *Mansfield Park* Mrs Rushworth removes 'herself, her maid, her footman, and her chariot, with true dowager propriety, to Bath'; but Mr Knightley (*Emma*) does 'not use his carriage so often as became the owner of Donwell Abbey'. The novels and letters also refer to several types of coach and carriage. Miss de Bourgh (in *Pride and Prejudice*) has a phaeton, a lightweight, four-wheeled carriage, with or without a top, drawn by two horses. Mrs Gardiner wants 'a low phaeton, with a nice little pair of ponies', and Jane Austen enjoyed a solitary drive in a phaeton during a visit to London. Open carriages with two wheels were either curricle, gig or tandem, each with a seat for the driver plus one passenger, and possibly a groom's seat behind. Several of the gentlemen characters drive curricles; Mr Thorpe (*Northanger Abbey*) enthuses over his, as a young man today might boast of a sports car: 'Curricle-hung, you see; seat, trunk, sword-case, splashing-board, lamps, silver moulding, all you see complete; the iron work as good as new or better' – and all for fifty guineas. One-horse gigs could be driven at reckless speed, which no doubt gave Mr Thorpe much pleasure.

The standard family carriage was the chaise, a four-wheeled, closed carriage guided by a post boy, or postilion. The chaise was suitable for taking parties to dinner and dances, and for journeys of a moderate distance. For long cross-country travel the post chaise was more appropriate. Travelling post generally meant changing chaises and transferring luggage at each post, unless the traveller owned the chaise. The seats inside a chaise faced the driver, as compared to a coach, in which the seats faced each other. A chariot was a closed, four-wheeled carriage with the addition of a driver's box, in which the single inside seat faced the driver.

The barouche, barouche-landau and landaulette were all open carriages set on four wheels, with various styles of collapsible top and two facing seats. Henry Crawford provides his barouche to take the Mansfield party on a day's outing to Sotherton Court, a distance of ten miles. The landaulette, as driven by Mr Wentworth in *Persuasion*, had only one seat.

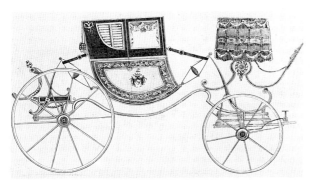

Chandos Leigh, a distant cousin of Jane Austen, obtained an estimate for a fashionable landau in 1829: the price of the basic carriage was £250, which included 'plate glass and mahogany shutters to the lights, and plated or brass bead to the leather, lined with best second cloth, cloth squabs, and worsted lace ... the body and carriage to be painted and picked out to order, and the panels highly varnished and polished, the whole of the best materials and workmanship'. Carriage-work, like cabinet-making, required the skills of an artist, and in its more ostentatious form involved veneering, inlay and decorative paintwork. The 'extras' required by Chandos Leigh included 'armorial bearings painted on the panels, barouche seat attached to the fore end of the body, a pair of hind standards and footman's cushion, morocco sleeping cushions, steps welted with morocco, silk spring curtains and venetian blinds in lieu of mahogany shutters, embossed crest, head, plates, embossed door handles, 2 full plated lamps or jappaned black'. These and other extras brought the total cost to £417.11.6; a 7 ½ per cent discount was allowed if it was paid for on completion, and one quarter of the total amount in exchange for a new carriage in five years. In contribution to the price, £60 was allowed 'for the old Chariot with all such things as belonged to it'.

Gentlemen only occasionally travelled by public coach, and ladies even less. Mrs Bennet supposes that Mr Darcy did not converse with Mrs Long because she 'does not keep a carriage, and had come to the ball in a hack chaise'. In *Mansfield Park*, Edmund Bertram arrives in Portsmouth 'by the mail', but he, Fanny and Susan Price return to Mansfield in a chaise. Mail coaches had armed guards, four inside passengers and no outside passengers, thereby providing greater comfort and speed than ordinary stagecoaches. One of the rare instances when Jane Austen was obliged to travel by public transport occurred in 1814; her journey was between Chawton and London in a public coach known as the Yalden.

I had a very good Journey, not crouded, two of the three taken up at Bentley being Children, the others of reasonable size; & they were all very quiet & civil. – We were late in London, from being a great Load and from changing Coaches at Farnham, it was nearly 4 I beleive when we reached Sloane St; Henry himself met me, & as soon as my

*Travellers who could not arrange their journey around visits to relatives or friends were forced to submit to the inconvenience of inns and hotels. Jane Austen often attended balls held in the Assembly rooms of the Angel Hotel in Basingstoke.*

Trunk & Basket could be routed out from all the other Trunks & Baskets in the World, we were on our way to Hans Place in the Luxury of a nice large cool dirty Hackney Coach. There were 4 in the Kitchen part of Yalden – & I was told 15 at top. . . .

Staying with friends was preferable to nights spent in inns and hotels, so the route of one's journey often accorded with the displacement of one's friends and relatives. For the Austens, the path between Godmersham Park in Kent and the Austens' home in Hampshire usually included a few days in either direction at the home of Henry Austen in London, a diversion which also put the travellers on a good stretch of main road.

In addition to the discomfort of journeys over sometimes uncertain roads was the possibility of mishap. A close friend of Jane Austen's was killed in a carriage accident, which is perhaps why she chose to open *Sanditon* with a serious accident. Edward Austen Knight injured a leg when his horse bolted, upsetting his carriage in the midst of Canterbury traffic,

*Bad weather could add considerably to the discomfort endured by coach travellers – and also to the time taken for a particular journey.*

*The high-spirited atmosphere of the age of coach travel is powerfully conveyed in this detail from Pollard's painting of the* North Country Mails at the Peacock, *1821.*

and in a letter of 1811 Jane mentions a fright received by herself and Eliza Austen when the horses 'gibbed' near London's Hyde Park Gate: 'a load of fresh gravel made it a formidable Hill to them, and they refused the collar; – I believe there was a sore shoulder to irritate. – Eliza was frightened, & we got out – & were detained in the Even$^g$ air several minutes.'

Nevertheless, with the installation of turnpikes, whereby road-users paid for the upkeep of the road, the quality of main roads greatly improved, and after 1793 main roads were provided with milestones for the first time since the days of the Romans. To Mr Darcy (*Pride and Prejudice*) fifty miles of good road was 'little more than half a day's journey', and Mrs Elton (*Emma*) boasted 'what is distance, Mr Weston, to people of large fortune? – You would be amazed to hear how my brother, Mr Suckling, sometimes flies about. You will hardly believe me – but twice in one week he and Mr Bragge went to London and back again with four horses'. This was a distance of five hundred miles.

This age of travel was celebrated in high-spirited manner by the gentlemen coachmen who drove four-in-hand at break-neck speeds between London and the coaching station at Salt Hill, where a sumptuous dinner awaited them.

# *Entertaining at home and the pleasures of food and wine*

When the fashionable season for enjoying the amusements of London, Bath and the coastal resorts was past, pleasures nearer home beckoned. Among the delights of owning a great country estate staffed by a legion of domestic servants were the ease and capacity of entertaining large numbers of guests. Life 'à la Godmersham', as Jane Austen referred to the comfortable routine of her brother's country seat in Kent, was similar to life in most country houses of the wealthy gentry, and included a daily round of visits from friends and relations, calling for tea and conversation. Other visitors extended their stay for a few days or weeks according to the length of their journey. Although main roads had improved, minor roads were still uncertain, and travellers usually had to put up with some discomfort on the way. For this reason visits of even a moderate distance customarily included a sojourn of several days and nights. Whenever Jane visited Godmersham Park her stay ran into several weeks.

Having guests at home was the only impetus required for organizing sumptuous dinner parties and evening entertainments, which might include cards, music and perhaps an impromptu ball. Such occasions required studious planning on the part of the hostess. Menus had to be discussed with the housekeeper and cooks, supplies checked, special items ordered from London shops, and seating arrangements considered. Bedrooms that had been shut up were opened and aired, chimneys swept and fires prepared, while the staff were put in readiness for receiving company. Musicians had to be booked for musical evenings or a ball, the latter requiring a discussion and perhaps instruction on the latest country dances. For home theatricals, costumes were improvised or selected from pattern books; directions were given to the seamstress, and masks were purchased.

Whenever guests were invited to dinner, the family's best china, crystal and plate would be conspicuously displayed. All the waking hours until dinner were referred to as the morning; thus dinner divided the day. In some rural districts it was not unusual to have this meal at three or four in the afternoon, but towards the turn of the century the dinner hour edged towards five or six, and in the early nineteenth century six-thirty or seven became very fashionable. On 18 December 1798, Jane wrote from Steventon to Godmersham: 'We dine now at half after three, & have done dinner I suppose before you begin. . . . I am afraid you will despise us.' But by 9 December 1808 she wrote 'we never dine now before 5'.

Just prior to dinner, family and guests in evening dress would gather in the drawing room for an interval of peremptory conversation, before proceeding to the dining room. In contemporary houses the drawing room was usually located at sufficient distance from the dining room to allow for some stateliness in the procession to table. Protocol dictated that the way would be led by the principal lady among the company; Elizabeth

Elliot in *Persuasion*, as the eldest daughter of a baronet, immediately follows Lady Russell out of the country's drawing rooms while in Highbury, and distinction of rank lays a similar requirement upon Mrs Elton, though she incorrectly makes reference to the situation: 'Must I go first? I really am ashamed of always leading the way' (*Emma*).

Protocol also dictated the seating arrangements. At Godmersham Park Aunt Jane Austen was placed at the lower end of the table among other aunts: 'We had a very pleasant Dinner, at the lower end of The table at least; the merriment was chiefly between Edw$^d$ Louisa, Harriot & myself (Godmersham to Southampton, 1808). Some aristocratic families could take the distinctions of rank to the measure of pomposity; the Duke and Duchess of Hamilton proceeded to dinner before their company, sat together at the upper end of the table, ate together off one plate, and drank to nobody beneath the rank of earl.

A formal dinner, as conducted in large households, consisted of two main courses plus a dessert course, of twelve to twenty-five covers each. The dishes on the table were symmetrically arranged according to a plan previously worked out by the cook. Most cookery books of the period contain sample drawings as guides to how the dishes should be laid out, so that the table would be 'covered without being crowded' (*The Experienced English Housekeeper, 1796*). Recipes were often designated as a 'corner dish', referring to their position on the table, or as a 'remove', meaning that they were to be taken away. The first course normally contained the soup, a remove, which would then be replaced by a fish. This course would also contain meat and game, sauces, vegetables and perhaps a sweet pudding. Following the first course the table would be completely relaid by the servants with diners present – which accounts for the uncomfortable interval during Emma's dinner with the Coleses: 'The conversation was here interrupted. They were called on to share in the awkwardness of a rather long interval between courses, and obliged to be as formal and orderly as the others. But when the table was again safely covered, when every corner dish was again exactly right.' The second course, lighter than the first, included several main dishes of meat and fish, but with a greater variety of puddings, creams and tarts. A menu of twenty-five dishes, of which Cassandra Austen partook, was provided for Prince William of Gloucester by the Dean of Canterbury in 1798. R. W. Chapman, in his edition of Jane Austen's letters, gives the bill of fare:

Salmon Trout
Soles
Fricando of Veal. Rais'd Giblet Pie
Vegetable Pudding
Chickens. Ham
Muffin Pudding
Curry of Rabbits. Preserve of Olives
Soup. Haunch of Venison
Open Tart Syllabub. Rais'd Jelly

> Three Sweetbreads, larded
> Maccaroni. Buttered Lobster
> Peas
> Potatoes
> Baskets of Pastry. Custards
> Goose

It was the custom for guests to help each other to choose from the nearest dishes, which gave the gentlemen an opportunity to show off their fine manners to the ladies on either side. Earlier in the century, ladies and gentlemen faced their opposite sex across the table, but towards the end of the century, and certainly in the early nineteenth century, the mode was to dine 'promiscuously': boy, girl, boy, girl.

Between courses, water in bowls was available so that mouths could be rinsed, or hands washed, as fingers were probably used as frequently as forks. If a dessert course was served, it was a feast for the eyes as well as the palate. The white linen tablecloth was removed, and the table relaid, with fruits and jellies and other sweetmeats attractively displayed in little dishes surrounding a pyramid of raised dishes. For festive celebrations, table decorations could be as simple as a sprinkling of rose petals or spring flowers across the cloth. At other times confectioners worked long hours, producing fantasy scenes of sugar cottages beside barley-sugar temples, with Neptunes and cockle shells sailing over looking-glass seas. These spectacles occasionally became so high and dense that guests were unable to see each other. Lord Albemarle's confectioner produced a tower of gods and goddesses rising upwards to a height of fifteen feet, but when it was time to dress the table, it was discovered that the display was too tall to fit into the room. However, apart from in the Prince Regent's banqueting hall, a more subtle display was the usual practice.

Following dessert, and perhaps a glass of wine, the ladies would withdraw to the drawing room while the gentlemen enjoyed more relaxed conversation with port and brandy. Eventually the gentlemen joined the ladies for tea or coffee, and cakes. Whereas earlier in the eighteenth century the lady of the house ceremoniously prepared tea for her guests, by the nineteenth century tea and coffee were made in the kitchen by the housekeeper and carried to the drawing room by the butler and footmen.

House guests could expect a light breakfast, usually served at ten o'clock, consisting of rolls, toast, tea, coffee or chocolate and perhaps some cheese. Stoneleigh Abbey offered a more substantial repast, as Mrs Austen described in her letter of 1806: 'Chocolate, coffee, Tea, Plum Cake, Hot Rolls, Cold Rolls, Bread, butter & dried toast for me'. As the interval between breakfast and dinner increased, luncheon was introduced, particularly for ladies, as gentlemen were likely to be engaged in business or sport – though Willoughby allowed himself a 'nuncheon' in *Sense and Sensibility*. Luncheon was generally a light meal of cold meat or sandwiches, the latter 'neatly cut in mouthfuls, so as to be taken up with a fork' (*The Complete Servant*, 1825). Incidental snacks were likely to be offered at any time as an emollient to unexpected social meetings or morning calls; such refreshments were offered to Elizabeth Bennet and her aunt and uncle at Pemberley: 'cold meat, cake, and a variety of all the finest fruits in season... beautiful pyramids of grapes, nectarines, and peaches' (*Pride and Prejudice*). Afternoon callers could expect to receive tea with crumpets, scones and biscuits, though afternoon tea did not become the national institution the English think of today until approximately the 1840s.

The cook was one of the highest paid and most prized members of the household staff. Mr Woodhouse (*Emma*), a fastidious eater with an anxious concern for his own and his company's digestions, boasted that 'Serle understands boiling an egg better than anybody'; she could even be trusted with pork, 'very thoroughly boiled'. In 1807 the Austens suffered the extended absence of 'Jenny', who did their cooking for them. Jane wrote from Southampton:

> I am glad I did not know beforehand that she was to be absent during the whole or almost the whole of our friends being with us, for though the inconvenience has not been nothing, I should have feared still more. Our dinners have certainly suffered not a little by having only Molly's head and Molly's hands to conduct them; she fries better than she did, but not like Jenny.

Henry Austen kept a French cook at Sloane Street, a substantial burden on the household budget which may have been the suggestion of his wife, the former Comtesse de Feuillide. Immigrant chefs from the noble houses of France were settling into the wealthy houses of England, and their services, though expensive, were much sought after. In spite of the wars with France, it was still held that the French were arbiters of all things fashionable, and anything French or influenced by France carried some status: Mrs Bennet thought Mr Darcy had 'two or three' French chefs 'at least (*Pride and Prejudice*). Menus from this period also listed several French dishes, and occasionally English fare received upmarket French names. The very English meat pie, for example, became 'pâté'.

During this period, when most women from the middle classes upwards could read, cookery books were plentiful, and recipes, or receipts, were exchanged among friends and relatives. Martha Lloyd, a lifelong friend of the Austens who became the wife of Admiral Francis Austen in 1828, lived with Mrs Austen, Jane and Cassandra at Southampton and Chawton; she collected recipes from friends and relatives which she recorded in a leather-bound book. The first half of the book contains 107 recipes devoted to cookery, as well as fruit and bramble wines, and 'Ginger Beer fit to drink in 24 hours'; home remedies, perfumery and household tips are included at the back. The recipes, probably dating from the late eighteenth century to the first quarter of the nineteenth century give instructions for soup, jellies, fish, fish sauces, for curing bacon and cooking ham, for preparing numerous 'made' dishes, roast vegetables, cheese dishes, vinegars, pickles, preserves and breads. Among the perfumery recipes are: 'Lavender Water', 'Cold Cream', 'Coral Tooth Powder', and

'Pot Pourie'. In the garden at Mansfield Park Fanny Price cut roses for drying, and at Godmersham Park Fanny Austen Knight and her mother prepared 'essence of rose and narcissus' from a recipe written by Fanny's friend Miss Chapman:

> We made some essence of rose and narcissus some time ago, but as mama is not quite satisfied with the smell, she would be much obliged to you to write out the whole process in case we should have forgotten anything & likewise to let you know if you *burnt a hole* in your pewter plate, as we did so, & therefore the *Cook* won't *let* us try again. (Godmersham Park, 15 July 1806)

It was in the still-room that cordials and other alcoholic liquors were distilled, as well as herbal tonics, remedies, floral essences and cosmetics.

In her correspondence and diaries Fanny Austen Knight mentions numerous entertainments enjoyed at Godmersham Park – birthday celebrations, masquerades, theatricals, balls and Christmas festivities. A birthday in the family meant overnight guests, an 'excellent' dinner followed by coffee, and then cards, which almost always involved a wager; on Fanny's birthday she generally 'won the pool'. On one birthday the company played 'Oranges and Limes, Hunt the Slipper, Wind the Jack and Lighting a candle in haste' followed by a 'nice ball until after 10'. The Georgians were fond of such games, many of which later became popular for children. More complex amusements, such as backgammon and anagrams, were popular, but none of these superseded cards for an evening's diversion. Whist and cribbage were played at Mansfield Park, and piquet and loo at Netherfield in *Pride and Prejudice*. Several other card games are mentioned in the novels and letters, most of them involving gambling. The stakes were relatively low within the family circle, though among the society of London and Bath gentlemen and ladies lost huge sums on reckless bets, bringing scandal and disgrace to their honoured families. Even local get-togethers sometimes involved uncomfortable wagers across the card table: 'On entering the drawing-room she found the whole party at loo, and was immediately invited to join them; but expecting them to be playing high, she declined it' (*Pride and Prejudice*).

Dancing was the other great amusement, whether conducted at home or in the neighbourhood assembly rooms. The party from Godmersham Park, which often included Jane or Cassandra Austen, frequently enjoyed the balls held at Ashford and Canterbury, while the young Austens of Steventon frequently attended assembly balls at Basingstoke, where for the price of a ticket they could enjoy country dances, mix with local society, and take tea and other refreshments. In 1809 the *Hampshire Chronicle* mentioned the annual assembly held at Alresford: 'Admission 3s 6d, tea 1s. Dancing to commence at 7 o'clock'. In 1817 Fanny Austen Knight wrote in her diary, 'Papa, Lizzie, Edward, William and I went to a Ball at Alresford – very select – good company, but not full'. For chaperons and others not inclined to dance there was card-playing in the room adjoining the ballroom. Young ladies were always chaperoned by an older couple or a married woman; Lydia Bennet commented 'Lord! How I should like to be married before any of you; and then I would chaperon you about to all the balls' (*Pride and Prejudice*).

Jane Austen mentions dancing twenty dances at one local ball and nine times out of ten at another, while taking note of the fashions, manners and gossip among the company. But in a recently discovered letter to her sister dated 8 January 1799, Jane describes a dance at which she was something of a wallflower:

> There were more dancers than the room could conveniently hold, which is good enough to constitute a good ball at any time. I do not think I was very much in request. . . . People were rather apt not to ask me till they could not help it; one's consequence, you know, varies so much at times without any particular reason. There was one Gentleman, an officer of the Cheshire, a very good looking young man who I was told wanted very much to be introduced to me; but as he did not want it quite enough to take much trouble in effecting it, we never could bring it about.

Formal balls, whether private or public, observed the precedence of the most important lady in opening the ball. In *Emma* the new bride Mrs Elton opens the ball at the Crown, while on one occasion at Goodnestone Park, Lady Bridges' fifth son Edward took Jane's hand and escorted her to the floor, inviting her, as guest of honour, to begin the ball. The opening dance was usually an old-fashioned minuet, all bows and curtseys; thereafter, sets of light-hearted country dancing were performed, in which couples faced one another in rows or formed circles. The quadrille, often mentioned by Jane Austen, was one of the most popular country dances of the early nineteenth century, as was the cotillion. During these dances couples were carefully watched to remain at arm's length, for although the waltz had begun to make an appearance on the Continent, England of the early nineteenth century thought it 'immoral'. Some private balls were informal, in which case music was provided by one of the ladies on the piano forte or perhaps by a fiddler got up from the servants' hall. Others involved more planning and more invitations: eighteen couples are mentioned in *Sense and Sensibility*, and in *Emma* five couples are thought insufficient: 'it will not do to *invite* five couples. It can be allowable only as the thought of a moment.' Grand occasions such as Lord Portsmouth's annual ball at Hurstbourne Park in Hampshire caused quite a stir in the Austen neighbourhood and required considerable preparation on the part of guests, in terms of looking one's fashionable best and arriving in elegant style. After the dancing an artfully arranged supper would be expected, as 'A private dance, without sitting down to supper, was pronounced an infamous fraud upon the rights of men and women' (*Emma*). At Godmersham Park, following the celebrations in honour of Fanny Austen Knight's fifteenth birthday, friends and family enjoyed 'Cold chicken cut up, Blanc Mange, jellies, Pastry, Celery, whipped syllabub etc. etc. most tastefully displayed'.

*The elaborate menus described in contemporary cookery books point to dinner parties as occasions of conspicuous consumption. Cooking was labour-intensive, requiring a vast army of kitchen staff, and great care was always taken with the presentation of dishes. Above left: Salmon with shrimp sauce. Above right: Sweetbreads and chicken fricassee. Opposite, above: Roast turkey, in the centre, with Florentine rabbits and beef olives. Opposite, below: Tongue with redcurrant sauce. All of these dishes were recreated from original eighteenth-century recipes.*

The Christmas season of Georgian England provided several opportunities for convivial entertainment and gaiety. There is a tendency to link the origination of Yuletide festivities with Charles Dickens, when in fact the celebrated Victorian Christmas, so warmly depicted on later nineteenth-century Christmas cards, simply gave publicity to what was a firm English tradition and the cause of much merrymaking among upper-class households of the eighteenth and early nineteenth centuries. Indeed, the principal difference between the Georgian Christmas and that celebrated during Victorian times was the introduction of the Christmas tree by Albert, the Prince Consort.

In the novels and letters, Jane Austen's grown-up perspective on Christmas festivities is mostly restricted to food and drink, families and conversation. While Cassandra Austen was enjoying a splendid Christmas at Godmersham Park, Jane wrote to her of their somewhat patchy celebration at the Austens' Castle Square lodgings in Southampton, where the family had set up home between 1806 and 1809: 'The last hour, spent in yawning and shivering in a wide circle round the fire, was dull enough, but the tray had admirable success. The widgeon and the preserved ginger were as delicious as one could wish. But as to our black butter, do not decoy anybody to Southampton by such a lure, for it is all gone' (27 December 1808). Christmas at Uppercross (*Persuasion*) was a much jollier affair:

> Immediately surrounding Mrs Musgrove were the little Harvilles, whom she was sedulously guarding from the tyranny of the two children from the Cottage, expressly arrived to amuse them. On one side

was a table occupied by some chattering girls, cutting up silk and gold paper; and on the other were trestles and trays, bending under the weight of brawn and cold pies, where riotous boys were holding high revel; the whole completed by a roaring Christmas fire, which seemed determined to be heard in spite of all the noise of the others. Charles and Mary also came in, of course, during their visit, and Mr Musgrove made a point of paying his respects to Lady Russell, and sat down close to her for ten minutes, talking with a very raised voice, but from the clamour of the children on his knees, generally in vain. It was a fine family piece.

In *Emma* Mr John Knightley's Scrooge-like attitude towards setting out on a journey of three-quarters of a mile for Christmas Eve dinner at the Randalls – 'going in dismal weather, to return probably in worse; four horses and four servants taken out for nothing but to convey five idle shivering creatures into colder rooms and worse company than they might have had at home' – is in sharp contrast to the slightly tipsy Mr Elton's remark: 'At Christmas everybody invites their friends about them, and people think little of even the worst weather. I was snowed up at a friend's house once for a week. Nothing could be pleasanter. I went for only one night, and could not get away till that very dayse' night.'

At Godmersham Park, where Cassandra Austen was wont to spend the festive season, the celebrations were pure enchantment. The diaries and letters of Fanny Austen Knight are filled with vivid images of Godmersham's holiday entertainments, conveyed with a tinge of child-like wonder. In December 1808 Fanny describes the 'amusements', which began with the arrival of family and friends on Christmas Eve. Having taken tea with young Fanny, the company prepared for the evening, which was highlighted with

> a delightful Ball ... which began at 7, ended at 10. We had 12 dances & sometimes 5, 6 or 7 couples at different times. I danced 9 and played 3 – we then had a game of Hunt the Slipper and ended the day with sandwiches and tarts. ... I must not omit saying that the little ones dressed up as usual and sang Christmas Carols.

On Christmas Day the children of Godmersham Park were given 'Christmas Boxes' containing money; Fanny received '2 guineas' in hers. After their breakfast, the younger children sang carols in the servants' hall, while the older ones, 'Fanny, Edward, George and Henry', looked forward to joining the adults in the dining parlour for a sumptuous Christmas dinner at the early hour of four o'clock. During the evening the servants were often invited to join the company in a toast to the season, with the children again singing carols, though this time in expectation of receiving money that was later to be given to the poor.

From Christmas Day until Twelfth Night Fanny mentions 'different amusements every evening! We had Bullet Pudding, then Snap-dragon,

& ... we danced or played at cards'. In describing a 'Bullet Pudding' to her friend Miss Chapman, she wrote:

> I was surprised that you did not know what a Bullet Pudding is but as you don't I will endeavour to describe it as follows: You must have a large pewter dish filled with flour which you must pile up into a sort of pudding with a peak at top, you must then lay a Bullet at top & everybody cuts a slice of it & the person that is cutting it when the Bullet falls must poke about with their *nose* & chins till they find it & then take it out with their mouths which makes them strange figures all covered with flour but the worst is that you must not *laugh* for fear of the flour getting up your nose & mouth & choking you. You must not use your hands in taking the *Bullet* out.

On the evening of 5 January 1809 the party was 'collected together' for 'several little dances to Aunt L's playing, and before she came I was the performer and of course did not get much dancing'. But Fanny made up for this deficiency when 'blind John who used to perform at the Servants Balls' was sequestered, and the company enjoyed twelve dances.

'Twelfth day' 1806 was perhaps the most delightful of the Christmas festivities at Godmersham Park:

> On Twelfth day we were all agreeably surprised with a sort of masquerade, all being dressed in character, & then we were conducted into the library which was all lighted up & at one end a throne was surrounded with a Grove of Orange Trees & other shrubs & all this was totally unknown to us all! Was not it delightful & I should have liked you very much to have been at the party.

Masquerade was popular as a public entertainment during the eighteenth century, and a particular passion of Horace Walpole. His description of the masquerade held at Ranelagh pleasure gardens in 1749 suggests that the Austen Knights may have borrowed some of their ideas from that fairytale setting, though in fact Ranelagh was closed in 1803.

> When you entered, you found the whole garden filled with Masks, and spread with tents, which remained all night *very commodely*.... On the canal was a sort of gondala, filled with music, rowing about. All around the outside of the amphitheatre were shops filled with Dresden china, japan, etc, and all the shopkeepers in mask. The amphitheatre was illuminated, and in the middle was a circular bower composed of all kinds of firs in tubs, from twenty to thirty feet high: under them orange-trees, with the finest auriculas in pots; and festoons of natural flowers hanging from tree to tree. Between the arches too were firs, the smaller ones in the balconies above. There were booths for tea and wine, gaming tables and dancing, and about two thousand persons. In short it pleased me more than anything I ever saw.

Costumes in the character of a shepherdess, Turk, Harlequin, historical figure or the opposite sex were favourites of the eighteenth century and,

Opposite: *A table set for dessert: the George III glass tazza holds fresh fruit and jelly or syllabub – a particular favourite of the era. The pineapple, a costly fruit, was a symbol of hospitality. The tablecloth was always removed for dessert.*

*'Maids of Honour' and syllabub decorated with violets create an appetizing spread.*

apparently, at Godmersham Park. For a 'masquerade' held on 6 January 1809 the Godmersham party 'got some Masks at Canterbury':

> & after Dessert [Aunt Louisa], who was the only person to know the characters … took one by one out of the room, & having equipped them, put them into separate rooms, & lastly dressed herself. We were then all conducted into the library & performed our different parts. Papa & the little ones from Lizzy downward knew nothing of it & it was so well managed that none of the characters knew one another.…
> Aunt Louisa & L Deedes were Dominos, F Cage Frederica Flirt (which she did excellently), M Deedes, Orange Woman; Mama, Shepherdess; self, Fortuneteller, Edward … beau; G, Irish postboy, Henry, watchman, William, harlequin; we had such frightful masks, that it was enough to kill one with laughing at putting them on & altogether it went off very well & quite answered our expectations.

A 'Domino' was a Venetian disguise of a black cloak with a hood and a grotesque white mask worn with a three-cornered hat. 'I have found a little unmasked moment to write to you,' Horace Walpole wrote to a friend in 1740, 'but for this week I have been so muffled up in my domino, that I have not had the command of my elbows.'

A masquerade was actually a play within a play, in which the roles were heightened by costume, requiring the players to act up to their characters. In *Mansfield Park* Jane Austen uses a home theatrical metaphori-

*These Chelsea figurines portray popular masquerade costumes of the period. On the left is a 'Turk' and on the right a shepherdess. Both disguises were among those worn by Christmas revellers at Godmersham Park in 1809.*

cally to mask emotions too tender for sharing off-stage – an acceptable ruse to the theatre-going Georgians, who loved acting, plays and players. *Lovers' Vows* was the play intended to be performed on the stage built in the billiard room at Mansfield Park. The dining room of Steventon Rectory was used for staging the Austens' plays during Christmas, and in the summer the rectory barn was their theatre, which saw such performances as Sheridan's *The Rivals* and Thomas Francklin's tragedy *Matilda*. During the Christmas holiday at Godmersham Park the party acted out a bill of 'select pieces'. The servants were invited, and 'the company sat by the curtains in the breakfast parlour'.

> So we had a very good stage. Miss Sharp contrived the dresses and they were admirable! Nothing could be better suited. First George repeated a Prologue, then came 'Alfred a Drama', then An appropriate Address by Lizzy; 'Pride Punished or Innocence Rewarded', a little piece of Miss Sharp's. Duchess, George; Flora, a shepherdess. F Cage, fairy; Serena, myself. The Prologue to Barbarossa, – Edward, the 1st scene – Act of Douglas, Lord Randolph – G; Norval – E, Lady R myself; the whole concluded with 'The Cits Country Box' by Fanny Catherine Austen. I forgot 'The Fairy's [?]' by Lizzy next to 'Pride Punished'. It was a delightful evening and everybody seemed pleased.

In writing to her sister Cassandra, who was enjoying Christmas at Godmersham in 1801, Jane Austen expressed a kind of smug pleasure in thinking that even their pretentious cousin Philadelphia Walter would have been satisfied with the programme of 'Christmas Gaieties' at Godmersham Park.

# *Epilogue*

ANE AUSTEN'S ENGLAND, and the society in which she
lived during the latter years of the eighteenth century and the
early years of the nineteenth, was a world of privilege – the
privilege of rank and social position, of vast fortunes and
influential connections. Yet it was also a world in the process of rapid evolution. With the changing distribution of wealth and increasing social
mobility, land and money were no longer clear indications of status, and
ever greater emphasis was therefore laid on the qualities that distinguished a 'true' gentleman, regardless of pedigree: a polished ease and
politeness of manner, a capacity for poised and informed discourse on a
variety of subjects, and a discerning appreciation of the arts. Even ladies
were encouraged to exert themselves in acquiring these cultured sensibil-
ities, becoming learned and conversant companions to their male
counterparts, in whose households they had previously been relegated to
the position of decorative accessory.

Young men and women of the period emerged into a world in which
there was much for such cultivated minds to appreciate. At the time of
Jane Austen's birth, in the reign of George III, Britain was enjoying a
Golden Age in domestic architecture, landscape design, furniture-making
and porcelain manufacture. Adam and Nash, Repton and Brown, among
others, were creating a legacy of great country houses set in artfully composed landscapes. Designed and built to endure generation upon generation, these imposing mansions provide a lasting reminder of the solid
values and achievements of the age. Within, they were appointed with
exciting new textiles, carpets and wallpapers, furnished with exquisitely
crafted pieces by Chippendale, Hepplewhite and Sheraton, and adorned
with elegant pottery and porcelain ornaments by Worcester, Wedgwood
and Chelsea – names that retain their prestige and popularity two centuries later. Even dress was undergoing considerable stylistic innovations,
as the stiff, structured fashions of the early eighteenth century gave way to
more natural, flowing lines, heightened by richly detailed accessories.
The taste for simplicity, for relaxed yet tailored elegance, was to set the
pace for fashion down to the present day.

Perhaps the most endearing feature of the Georgians, however, was
their capacity for enjoying themselves. Whether amid the fashionable elegance of a season in London, the varied delights of spa towns and coastal

resorts, or through dining and dancing at the lavish entertainments laid on at country houses, they exploited every opportunity for the social display of their cultivated manners.

This world of supremely civilized and pleasurable perfection was poised on the brink of unprecedented change, brought about, for the most part, by the Industrial Revolution. The conspicuous consumption of the richly appointed drawing rooms and well-stocked kitchens of the wealthy contrasted vividly with the realities of life for those at the lower end of the social scale – a contrast that would intensify as the Victorian age drew on. Yet the enduring memory of the period is as a time of dazzling creative genius and aesthetic achievement, which, in spite of greater resources, an increased population and mass education, has not since been matched. The brilliance of the era shines through to us today, not only in the fine houses and picturesque gardens of the period, but also in our modern homes, in which Georgian designs are now being revived – a fine tribute to the period's great architects, craftsmen and interior designers. Above all, the spirit of the age endures through the novels of Jane Austen, underlining the timeless talent of this great writer, who continues to give us pleasure to this day.

# Jane Austen's Life: A Chronology

1775  Born 16 December at Steventon Rectory, Hampshire.

1782  Jane is sent to Mrs Crawley's school in Oxford with her sister Cassandra and their cousin Jane Cooper.

1783  They move to Southampton, where Mrs Crawley's school has been relocated.

1785–c.1787  Jane and Cassandra are at Mrs Latournelle's Abbey School in Reading.

1790  Jane writes *Love and Friendship*, a farcical novel in the form of letters.

1791  The *History of England*, with illustrations by Cassandra.

1792  *Lesley Castle* is followed by other compositions.

1796–97  *First Impressions*, later entitled *Pride and Prejudice*.

1797  *Elinor and Marianne*, later entitled *Sense and Sensibility*. *First Impressions* is rejected for publication.

1797–98  *Susan*, later entitled *Northanger Abbey*.

1801  The Austen family move from Steventon to Bath.

1802  Offer of marriage from Harris Bigg-Wither, which Jane initially accepts but refuses the next day.

c.1803  Jane writes an unfinished novel, *The Watsons*. *Susan* is sold to the publishers Crosby & Co.

c.1805  *Lady Susan*

1805  Death of Jane's father, the Revd George Austen, in Bath on 21 January.

1806  The Austen family move from Bath to Southampton.

1809  Removal of the family from Southampton to the cottage at Chawton, where they are joined by Martha Lloyd. Attempt to secure publication of *Northanger Abbey*.

1811  *Sense and Sensibility* published by Thomas Egerton.

1813  *Pride and Prejudice* published by Egerton.

1814  *Mansfield Park* published by Egerton.

1815–16  *Persuasion*

1816  *Emma* published by John Murray. Manuscript and copyright of *Northanger Abbey* released by Crosby & Co.

1817  The uncompleted draft of *Sanditon* written. Jane moves to Winchester for medical treatment. Composition of verses on St Swithin on 15 July, shortly before her death from Addison's disease on 18 July. Jane is buried in the north aisle of Winchester Cathedral on 24 July.

1818  *Northanger Abbey* and *Persuasion* are published posthumously by Jane's brother, the Revd Henry Austen.

# A Directory of Georgian Designs

∾∾∾∾∾∾∾∾∾∾∾∾∾∾∾∾∾∾∾∾∾∾∾∾∾∾∾∾∾∾∾∾∾∾∾

## MUSEUMS AND HOUSES

*UK*
The museums and houses listed below contain collections of period rooms, furniture, fittings and artefacts. For more detailed information consult *Museums and Art Galleries in Great Britain and Ireland*, published annually by ABC Historic Publications; the *Directory of Museums and Living Displays*, by Kenneth Hudson and Ann Nicholls, published by M. Stockton Press; *The World of Learning*, published by Europa Publications Ltd; *Museums Yearbook 1989–90*; and the *Cambridge Guide to the Historic Places of Britain and Ireland.*

Abbey House Museum and Temple Newsam House
Leeds
West Yorkshire LS5 3GH
(0532) 641358/755821

Arbury Hall
Nuneaton
Warwickshire
(0203) 382804

Arlington Court
Barnstaple
Devon EX31 4LP
(027182) 296

Ashridge
Berkhamsted
Hertfordshire
(044284) 3491

Attingham Park
Shrewsbury
Shropshire
(074377) 203

Bethnal Green Museum of Childhood
Cambridge Heath Road
London E2
(081) 980 2415
*Children's furniture, toys, costume*

Blaise Castle House and Museum
Henbury, Bristol
Avon
(0272) 506789

British Museum
Great Russell Street
London WC1
(071) 636 1555

Central Museum and Art Gallery
Guildhall Road
Northampton
(0604) 34881

Chatsworth
Bakewell
Derbyshire
(024688) 2204

Chicheley Hall
Newport Pagnell
Buckinghamshire
(023065) 252

Chiswick House
Chiswick
London W4
(081) 995 0508

City Museum and Art Gallery
Bethesda Street
Hanley
Stoke-on-Trent
(0782) 202173

Dawlish Museum
The Knowle, Barton Terrace
Dawlish, Devon

Dodington House
Chipping Sodbury
Avon

Erddig (and gardens)
Wrexham
Clwyd

Fairlynch Arts Centre and Museum
27 Fore Street
Budleigh, Salterton
Devon EX9 6NG
(03954) 2666
*A marine cottage orné*

Finchcocks
Goudhurst
Kent
(0580) 211702
*Historic keyboard instruments in an 18th C house*

Geffrye Museum
Kingsland Road
London E2
(071) 739 9893
*Furniture*

The Georgian House
7 Great George Street
Bristol
Avon BS1 5RR
(0272) 299771

The Georgian House
7 Charlotte Square
Edinburgh
(031) 2252160

Gloucester City Museum and Art Gallery
Brunswick Road
East Gate Street
Gloucester
(0452) 24131

Goodwood House
Goodwood
Chichester
West Sussex PO18 0PX
(0243) 774107

Jane Austen's House
Chawton, Alton
Hampshire GU34 1SD
(0420) 83262

Kelmarsh Hall
Nr Market Harborough
Northamptonshire
(060128) 276

Kenwood House
Hampstead Lane
London
(081) 348 1286

Leeds City Museum
Calverley Street
Leeds
(0532) 462632

Manchester City Art Gallery
Mosley Street
Manchester
(061) 2369422

Moccas Court
Moccas
Hereford and Worcester
(09817) 381

Mompessen House
'Choristers' Green
Cathedral Close
Salisbury
Wiltshire
(0722) 335659

Museum of Social History
27 Kings Street
Kings Lynn
Norfolk
(0553) 775004

Pitshanger Manor Museum
Mattock Lane
Ealing
London W5
(081) 567 1227 / 579 2424,
ext. 42683

Preston Manor (The Thomas
Stanford Museum)
Preston Park
Brighton, East Sussex BN1 6SD
(0273) 63005

Ragley Hall
Alcester
Warwickshire B49 5NJ
(0789) 762090

No. 1 Royal Crescent
Bath
Avon BA1 2LR
(0225) 28126

Royal Pavilion
Brighton
East Sussex BN1 1UE
(0273) 603005

Saltram House
Plympton, Plymouth
Devon
(0752) 336546

Sezincote House
Nr Morton-in-Marsh
Gloucestershire

Sir John Soane's Museum
13 Lincoln's Inn Fields
London WC2
(071) 405 2107

Stoneleigh Abbey
Kenilworth
Warwickshire
(0926) 52116

Strangers' Hall Museum of
Domestic Life
Charing Cross
Norwich
Norfolk NR4
(0603) 667229

Syon House
Syon Park
Brentford, Middlesex TW8 8JF
(081) 560 0881

Victoria and Albert Museum
Cromwell Road
London SW7
(071) 938 8315

The Vyne
Sherborne St John
Basingstoke
Hampshire RG26 5DX
(0256) 881337

*FRANCE*
Musée des Arts Décoratifs
Palais du Louvre
Pavillon de Marsan
107 rue de Rivoli
75001 Paris, Seine
(1) 42 60 32 14

Musée Hermès
24 rue du Faubourg-Saint-
Honoré
75008 Paris, Seine
(1) 42 65 21 60

Musée de l'Impression sur
Etoffes de Mulhouse
3 rue des Bonnes-gens
68100 Mulhouse
(89) 45 51 20

*USA*
For more detailed information,
and additional houses and
museums, consult *The Official
Museum Directory*, published
annually in the USA by the
National Register Publishing
Company.

Ash Lawn-Highland
Albemarle County Route 795
Charlottesville, Virginia 22901
(804) 293-9539

Boston Museum of Fine Arts
465 Huntington Avenue
Boston, Massachusetts 02115
(617) 267-9300

Cincinnati Art Museum
Eden Park
Cincinnati, Ohio 45202
(513) 721-5204

Colonial Williamsburg
Foundation
POB C
Williamsburg, Virginia 23187
(804) 229-1000

Concord Museum
200 Lexington Road
Concord, Massachusetts 01742
(508) 369-9763

Cooper-Hewitt Museum
Smithsonian Institution's
National Museum of Design
2 East 91st Street
New York, New York 10128
(212) 860-6868

Drayton Hall
3380 Ashley River Road
Highway 61
Charleston
South Carolina 29414
(803) 766-0188

M.H. de Young Memorial
Museum
Golden Gate Park
San Francisco, California 94118
(415) 750-3600

Hammond Museum
Deveau Road of Route 124
North Salem, New York 10560
(914) 669-5033

Historic Charleston Foundation
51 Meeting Street
Charleston
South Carolina 29401
(803) 723-1623

Kenmore
1201 Washington Avenue
Fredericksburg, Virginia 22401
(703) 373-3381
*Plasterwork and colonial kitchen*

Los Angeles County Museum of
Art
5905 Wilshire Boulevard
Los Angeles 90036
(213) 857-6000

Mary Washington House
1200 Charles Street
Fredericksburg, Virginia 22401
(703) 373-1569

The Metropolitan Museum of
Art
Fifth Avenue at 82nd Street
New York, New York 10028
(212) 879-5500

Monticello
P.O. Box 316
Charlottesville, Virginia 22902
(804) 293-2158

Mount Vernon
End of George Washington
Parkway South
Mount Vernon, Virginia 22121
(703) 780–2000

Museum of the City of New York
Fifth Avenue at 103rd Street
New York, New York 10029
(212) 534–1672

The Redwood Library and
Athenaeum
50 Bellvue Avenue
Newport, Rhode Island 02840
(401) 847–0179
*Oldest American library in continuous
use – collection of 18th C pattern
books and books on architecture, design
& ornaments*

Shelburne Museum
Route 7
Shelburne, Vermont
(804) 985–3346

Sherwood Forest Plantation
Route 5 to Richmond &
Williamsburg
Charles City, Virginia 23020
(804) 829–5377

Shirley Plantation
501 Shirley Plantation Road
Charles City, Virginia 23030
(804) 795–2385

Wilton House Museum
South Wilton Road
Richmond, Virginia 23226
(804) 282–5936

Winterthur Museum and
Gardens
Winterthur
Delaware 19735
(302) 888–4600

Woodlawn Plantation
9000 Richmond Highway
Alexandria, Virginia 22121
(703) 780–4000

Yale Center for British Art
1080 Chapel Street
New Haven, Connecticut 06520
(203) 432–2800

## Gardens

*UK*
Blaise Castle House and
Museum
Henbury, Bristol
Avon
(0272) 506789
*Repton*

Bowood House
Calne
Wiltshire
(0249) 812102
*Brown and Repton*

Chiswick House
Chiswick
London W4
(081) 995 0508
*Kent*

Deans Court
Wimborne
Dorset
*18th C kitchen garden*

Museum of Garden History
St Mary-at-Lambeth
Lambeth Palace Road
London SE1 7JU
(071) 261 1891

Norton Conyers
Ripon
North Yorkshire
(076584) 333
*Walled garden specializing in 18th C
plants*

Sezincote House and Gardens
Nr Morton-in-Marsh
Gloucestershire
*Influenced Repton*

Stourhead
Stourton, Warminster
Wiltshire
(0747) 840348
*Composed view of lake, bridge, temple
and village*

West Wycombe Park
High Wycombe
Buckinghamshire
(0494) 24411
*18th C Garden temples*

*USA*
Afton Villa
St Francisville
Louisiana
(504) 635–6330 (Tourist
Information)

Magnolia Plantation and
Gardens
Route 4
Charleston
South Carolina 29414
(803) 571–1266

Monticello
P.O. Box 316
Charlottesville, Virginia 22902
(804) 293–2158

Mount Vernon
End of George Washington
Parkway South
Mount Vernon, Virginia 22121
(703) 780–2000

Rockwood Museum
610 Shipley Road
Wilmington, Delaware 19809
(302) 571–7776

Rosedown Plantation
St Francisville
Louisiana 70775
(504) 635–3332

## Kitchens

*UK*
Canons Ashby House
Canons Ashby, Daventry
Northamptonshire
(0327) 860044

The Georgian House
7 Charlotte Square
Edinburgh
(031) 2252160

Pickford House Museum
41 Friar Gate
Derby
(0332) 293111 ext. 402/782

Royal Pavilion
Brighton
East Sussex BN1 1UE
(0273) 603005

Saltram House
Plympton, Plymouth
Devon
(0752) 336546

Strangers' Hall Museum of
Domestic Life
Charing Cross
Norwich
Norfolk NR4
(0603) 667229

*USA*
Colonial Williamsburg
Foundation
POB C
Williamsburg, Virginia 23187
(804) 229–1000

Heyward-Washington House
87 Church Street
Charleston
South Carolina 29401
(803) 722–0354

Old Sturbridge Village
1 Old Sturbridge Road
Sturbridge, Massachusetts 01566
(508) 347–3362

Shelburne Museum
Route 7
Shelburne, Vermont
(802) 985–3346

Wilton Heritage Museum
249 Danbury Road
Wilton, Connecticut
(203) 762–7257
*Furnishings, accessories, costumes, kitchen utensils*

## FABRICS AND WALLPAPERS
*UK*

For more information on sources of 18th and early 19th C designs contact the London Interior Designers' Centre, 1 Crigle Street, London SW8, (071) 627 5000. Recommended reading: *New Decorator's Directory* by Lorraine Johnson / Michael Joseph / Design Council; Mermaid Books 1986.

The Archive Printing Company Ltd
Houldsworth Mill
Houldsworth Street
Stockport
Cheshire
(061) 4431428

Bennison Fabrics Ltd
91 Pimlico Road
London SW1
(071) 730 3370/8076

Colefax & Fowler
39 Brook Street
London W1
(071) 493 2231

H.A. Percheron Ltd
97–9 Cleveland Street
London W1
(071) 580 1192

Hamilton Weston Wallpapers
11 Townshend Road
Richmond, Surrey TW9 1XH
(081) 940 4850

Laura Ashley Decorator
Collection, *available in major cities throughout Europe and the UK*

Manuel Canovas Ltd
37–9 Cheval Place
London SW7
(071) 255 2298

Osborne & Little plc
304 Kings Road
London SW3
(071) 352 1456

Pallu & Lake Ltd *

Tissunique Ltd
'Historic Prints Collection' *

Zoffany Ltd
27a Motcomb Street
London SW1 8JU
(071) 235 5295/7241

*USA*
Baker Knapp & Tubbs *
917 Merchandise Mart
Chicago, Illinois 60654
(312) 329–9410

Bassett and Vollum Wallpapers
217 North Main Street
Galena, Illinois 61036
(815) 777–2460

Boussac of France Inc. *
979 Third Avenue
New York, New York 10022
(212) 838–7878

Brunschwig & Fils *
979 Third Avenue
New York, New York 10022
(212) 838–7878

Clarence House Fabrics Ltd *
211 East 58th Street
New York, New York 10011
(212) 752–2890

Greeff Fabrics Inc.
200 Garden City Plaza
Garden City, New York 11530
(516) 741–9440

Hinson & Company
8687 Melrose Avenue
#637
Los Angeles, California 90069
(213) 659–7075

Katzenbach & Warren Inc.
950 Third Avenue
New York, New York 10022
(212) 759–5410

Laura Ashley Decorator
Collection
979 Third Avenue
New York, New York 10022
(212) 223–0220

Manuel Canovas Inc.
136 East 57th Street
18th Floor
New York, New York 10022
(212) 486–9230

* *Available through leading interior designers*

Payne Fabrics *
3500 Kettering Blvd
Box 983
Dayton, Ohio 45401
(513) 293–4121

## Costume
*UK*
Details of museum booklets and illustrations which may be of interest can be found in: *Costume – A general bibliography* by Anthony Pegaret and Janet Arnold, published by the Costume Society in association with the Victoria and Albert Museum.

Abington Museum
Abington Park
Northampton
(0604) 31454

Bath Museum of Costume
Assembly Rooms
Bennett Street
Bath, Avon BA1 2QH
(0225) 461111

Bexhill Manor Costume
Museum
Manor House Gardens
Old Town
Bexhill-on-Sea
East Sussex TN39 3QU
(0424) 215361

Blaise Castle House and
Museum
Henbury, Bristol
Avon
(0272) 506789

Gloucester Folk Museum
West Gate Street
Gloucester
(0452) 26467

Killerton House
Nr Exeter
Devon
(0392) 881345

Manchester City Art Galleries
Mosley Street
Manchester
(061) 2369422

Northampton Central Museum
Guildhall Road
Northampton
(0604) 34881

Pitville Pumproom Museum
Gallery of Fashion
Pitville Park

Cheltenham
Gloucestershire GL52 3JE
(0242) 512740

Platt Hall
Platt Fields
Rusholme
Greater Manchester
(061) 2245217

Victoria and Albert Museum
Cromwell Road
London SW7
(071) 938 8315

*FRANCE*
Musée des Arts de la Mode et du
Costume
Pavillon de Maisan
rue de Rivoli
75001 Paris, Seine

Musée Cluny
6 place Paul-Painlevé
75005 Paris, Seine
(1) 43 25 62 00

Musée de la Mode et du
Costume
Palais Galliéra
10 ave Pierre Ier de Serbie
75116 Paris
(1) 47 20 85 23

*USA*
Boston Museum of Fine Arts
Department of Textiles and
Costume
465 Huntington Avenue
Boston, Massachusetts 02115
(617) 267–9300 ext. 536

Brooklyn Museum
200 Eastern Parkway
Brooklyn, New York 11238
(718) 638–5000

The Costume Institute at the
Phoenix Art Museum
1625 North Central Avenue
Phoenix, Arizona 85004
(602) 257–1880

Fashion Institute of Technology
227 West 27th Stret
New York, New York
(212) 760–7700

Los Angeles County Museum of
Art
5905 Wilshire Boulevard
Los Angeles, California 90036
(213) 857–6000

The Metropolitan Museum of
Art, Costume Institute
5th Avenue at 82nd Street
New York, New York 10028
(212) 570–3908

The National Museum of
American History at the
Smithsonian
Costume Division
Room 4202
12th and Constitution Avenue
SW
Washington, D.C. 20560
(202) 357–3185

The Philadelphia Museum of Art
Department of Costume and
Textiles
26th and Benjamin Franklyn
Parkway
Philadelphia, Pennsylvania
19101–7646
(215) 787–5404

**Useful Addresses**
*UK*
The Architectural Heritage
Society of Scotland
43b Manor Place
Edinburgh, EH3 7EB
(031) 225 9724

Architectural Salvage
Netley House
Gomshall, Surrey GU5 9QA
*Maintains an index of a variety of
architectural items*

British Decorators' Association
6 Haywra Street
Harrogate
North Yorkshire HG1 5BL
(0423) 67292/3
*Has members who specialize in period
decoration*

British Institute of Interior
Design
1c Devonshire Avenue
Beeston, Nottingham NG9 1BS
(0602) 223255

English Heritage
Quayside House
429 Oxford Street
London WIR 2HD
(071) 355 1303

The Georgian Group
37 Spital Square
London E1 6DY
(071) 377 1722

Heritage in Wales
Cadw Welsh Historical
Monuments
Brunel House
2 Fitzalan Road
Cardiff CF2 1UY
(0222) 465511

Historic Houses Association
Ebury Street
London SW1W 0LU
(071) 730 9419

The National Trust
36 Queen Anne's Gate
London SW1
(071) 222 7391

The National Trust for Scotland
5 Charlotte Square
Edinburgh EH2 4DU
(031) 2226 5922

*USA*
Costume Society of America
55 Edgewater Drive
P.O. Box 73
Earleville, Maryland 21919
(301) 276–2329

The Getty Conservation
Institute
4503 Glencoe Avenue
Marina del Rey, California
90292–6537
(213) 822–2299

National Register of Historic
Places
1100 L St NW, Suite 6111
Washington, D.C. 20005
(202) 343–9536

National Trust for Historic
Preservation in the United States
1785 Massachusetts Avenue NW
Washington, D.C. 20036
(202) 673–4000

# Bibliography

Asterisked works are especially useful and are, in some cases, relevant to more than one chapter.

## 1. A Society of Grace and Manners

Austen, Caroline. *Reminiscences.* Jane Austen Society, 1986

Austen Leigh, James. *Memoir of Jane Austen.* First published 1870; reissued 1987

Austen Leigh, J E. *Recollections Of The Early Days Of The Vine Hunt and of Its Founder William John Chute, Esq MP of the Vine together with brief notices of the Adjoining Hunts, by a Sexagenarian.* Spottiswoode & Co., 1865

Austen Leigh, Mary Augusta. *James Edward Austen Leigh, A Memoir By His Daughter.* 1911

Austen Leigh, Mary Augusta. *Personal Aspects of Jane Austen.* 1920

Botsford, Jay Barrett. *English Society In The Eighteenth Century, As Influenced From Overseas.* 1924

Brown, Ivor. *Jane Austen And Her World.* 1966

Burnett, T A J. *The Rise & Fall of a Regency Dandy.* 1981

*Cecil, David. *A Portrait Of Jane Austen.* 1986

*Chapman, R W. *Jane Austen's Letters.* 1932; rev. ed. 1959

*Chapman, R W. *Jane Austen Selected Letters 1796–1817.* 1985

*Craik, W A. *Jane Austen In Her Time.* 1969

Davies, Mervyn. *Warren Hastings.* 1935

*Edwards, Anne-Marie. *In The Steps of Jane Austen.* 1979, 1985

Fox, Celina and Aileen Ribeiro. *Masquerade.* Museum of London, 1983

Frazer, Flora. *The English Gentlewoman.* 1987

Freedman, Francine Susan. '"Ceremonies of Life", Manners in the Novels of Jane Austen'. PhD dissertation – Tufts University, 1975

*Grey, J David (ed). *The Jane Austen Handbook.* 1986

Grier, Sydney C. *The Letters of Warren Hastings to his Wife.*

Grosvenor Myer, Valerie. *Authors In Their Age/Jane Austen.* 1980

Heathcote, T A. 'The Royal Military Academy Sandhurst'. Sandhurst, Camberley, Surrey

*Hibbert, Christopher. *The English, A Social History 1066–1945.* 1988

Hill, Constance. *Jane Austen, Her Homes and Her Friends.* 1902

*Honan, Park. *Jane Austen, Her Life.* 1987

'Jane Austen 1775–1817'. Catalogue of an exhibition held in the King's Library, 9 Dec 1975 to 29 Feb 1976. The British Library Board, 1975

'Jane Austen's House'. Jane Austen Memorial Trust and Jarrold Colour Publications, 1988

Reports for 1955, 1961, 1963, 1964 and 1988. Published separately by the Jane Austen Society

*Collected Reports 1966–1975, 1976–1985.* Jane Austen Society

*Jenkins, Elizabeth. *Jane Austen, A Biography.* 1938; pbk 1987

*Lane, Maggie. *Jane Austen's England.* 1986

*Laski, Marghanita. *Jane Austen And Her World.* 1969; rev. ed. 1975

LeFaye, Deirdre. *Jane Austen: A Family Record.* 1989

Macaulay, Lord. *Critical And Historical Essays.* Vol. III, Longmans, Green and Co., London, 1895

Plumb, J H. *The First Four Georges.* 1956, 1987

Porter, Ray. *English Society in the Eighteenth Century.* 1982, 1988

Tanner, Tony. *Jane Austen.* 1986

Wilks, Brian. *Jane Austen.* 1988

## 2. The Country House

Brade-Birks, Rev S Graham. 'Jane Austen and Godmersham'. (Available from Maidstone and Ashford Libraries)

*Cook, Olive. *The English Country House, an Art and a Way of Life.* 1974; pbk 1984

Cruickshank, Don. *A Guide To The Georgian Buildings of Britain and Ireland.* 1985

Fleming, Laurence & Alan Gore. *The English Garden.* 1988

*Girouard, Mark. *Life In The English Country House.* 1978, 1980

Gotch, J A. *The English Home From Charles I to George IV, Its Architecture, Decoration and Garden Design.* 1918

Gotch, J A. *The Old Halls and Manor-Houses of Northamptonshire.* 1936

Greenwood, C. *History of Kent, Vol. I.* 1838

Hellyer, Arthur. 'Hand of Unknown Genius: Garden and Landscape At Cottesbrooke Hall, Northamptonshire'. *Country Life,* May 15 1986

Hussey, Christopher. 'Godmersham Park, Kent' – I, II, III. *Country Life,* Feb 16, 23; Mar 2 1945

Isham, Gyles and Bruce Bailey. 'Cottesbrooke Hall Revisited'. *Country Life,* Feb 19 1970

*Jaques, George. *Georgian Gardens, The Reign of Nature.* 1983

Kaines Smith, S C. 'Stoneleigh Abbey'. 1984

Learmont, David. 'The Georgian House'. The National Trust for Scotland. 1989

**Leigh, Agnes Elinor. *Stoneleigh Abbey.* Privately printed, 1919**

Leigh, William Austen and Montague George Knight. *Chawton Manor And Its Owners.* 1911

Nares, Gordon. 'Cottesbrooke Hall, Northamptonshire' – I, *Country Life,* Mar 17 1955

Nicolson, Nigel. *The National Trust Book of Great Houses of Britain.* 1983

Oswald, Arthur. 'Cottesbrooke Hall, Northamptonshire' – I, II. *Country Life,* Feb 15 1936

Pass, Anne. 'Godmersham's Pride'. *Kent Life,* Oct 1985

*Pevsner, Nikolaus. 'The Architectural Setting of Jane Austen's Novels'. Journal of the Warburg and Courtauld Institutes, 31, 1968, 404–22

Plumtre, George. 'Goodnestone Park'. Privately printed, 1979

Prosser, G F. *Select Illustrations of Hampshire.* J & A Arch, 61 Cornhill, London, 1833

*Repton, H., assisted by his son J. Adey Repton. *Fragments On The Theory And Practice of Landscape Gardening.* J Taylor, At The Architectural Library, London, 1816

Smithers, Sir David Waldron. *Jane Austen in Kent.* 1981

Temple, Nigel. 'In Search of The Cottage Picturesque; Some Origins And Destinations'. The Georgian Group Report and Journal, London 1988

Temple, Nigel. 'Pages from An Architect's Notebook'.

Proceedings, Hampshire Field Club Archaeological Society, 44, 1988, 95–100
*Woodforde, John. *Georgian Houses For All*. 1978; pbk 1985

**3. Interior Styles**

Ackermann, Rudolph. *The Repository of Arts, Literature, Commerce, Manufactures, Fashion and Politics*. R Ackerman, London, 1809–28
Amery, C. *Period Houses and their Details*. 1974
*Ashton, Helen. *Parson Austen's Daughter*. 1949
*Beard, Geoffrey. *The National Trust Book of English Furniture*. 1985
Chippendale, Thomas. *The Gentleman and Cabinet-Maker's Director*. Facsimile of 3rd ed. of 1762, 1962
Clabburn, Pamela. *Furnishing Textiles*. 1988
Cornforth, John. *English Interiors 1790–1848, The Quest For Comfort*. 1978
Fastnedge, Ralph. *Sheraton Furniture*. Published by Antique Collectors' Club, Baron Publishing, Woodbridge, Suffolk, 1983
*Fowler, John and John Cornforth. *English Decoration in the 18th Century*. 1974
Jourdain, M. *English Interiors in Smaller Houses 1660–1830*. 1923
*Lees-Milne, James. *The Age of Adam*. 1947
Miller, Judith and Martin. *Period Style*. 1989
*Savage, G. *Concise History of Interior Decoration*. 1966
Schoeser, Mary and Celia Rufey. *English and American Textiles From 1790 to the Present*. 1989
Sim, Andrew. 'True Colours'. *Traditional Homes*, Feb 1989
Tattersall, C E C. *A History of British Carpets*. 1934
*Thornton, Peter. *Authentic Decor, The Domestic Interior 1620–1920*. 1985
*Yarwood, Doreen. *English Interiors*. 1983

**4. Fashion – And Its Genteel Competitors**

Brooke, Iris. *English Children's Costume Since 1775*. 1930; reprinted 1978
*Byrde, Penelope. *A Frivolous Distinction*. Bath City Council, 1970; reprinted 1986

Byrde, Penelope. 'Museum of Costume'. Bath City Council, 1987
*Carter, Alison J. *Regency to Art Nouveau: Taste and Fashion in European Jewellery from the Eighteenth to the Twentieth Centuries*. Cheltenham Art Gallery and Museums, 1986
Cumming, Valerie. *Exploring Costume History 1500–1900*. 1981
Ginsburg, Madeleine. *An Introduction to Fashion Illustration*. 1982
Hart, Avril D. 'English Men's Fashionable Dress 1600–1799'. Victoria and Albert Museum
Hill, Margot Hamilton and Peter A Bucknell. *The Evolution of Fashion, 1066 to 1930*. 1987
Osborne, Harold (ed). *The Oxford Companion to the Decorative Arts*. 1985
Rothstein, Natalie (ed). *Barbara Johnson's Album of Fashions and Fabrics*. 1987.
Rothstein, Natalie. *Silk Designs of the Eighteenth Century*. 1990.
Sichel, Marion. *The Regency*. 1978; reprinted 1987
Swan, June. *Shoes*. 1986
The Victoria and Albert Colour Books. *Patterns For Textiles*. 1986
The Victoria and Albert Colour Books. *Rococo Silks*. 1985

**5. In Pursuit of Entertainment**

Acworth, Margaretta. *Georgian Cookery*. Edited by Alice and Frank Prochaska, 1987
Adams, Samuel and Sarah. *The Complete Servant*. 1825; ed. Ann Haly, Southover Press, Lewes, 1989
Aylett, Mary and Olive Ordish. *First Catch Your Hare*. 1965
Ayrton, Elisabeth. *The Cookery of England*. 1974
*Burton, E. *The Georgians at Home 1714–1830*. 1967
*Chancellor, E. Beresford. *Life in Regency and Victorian Times 1800–1850*. 1927
Doran, John. *Table Traits*. Richard Bentley, London, 1854
Farley, John. *The London Art of Cookery*. 1783; ed. Ann Haly , Southover Press, Lewes, 1988
Glasse, Hannah. *The Art of Cookery Made Plain and Easy*. A facsimile of the first ed.1747. Prospect Books Ltd, London, 1983

Godden, Geoffrey A. *An Illustrated Encyclopedia of British Pottery and Porcelain*. 1989
Hickman, Peggy. *A Jane Austen Household Book*.
*Lane, Maggie. *A Charming Place*. 1988
*Margetson, Stella. *Leisure And Pleasure In The Eighteenth Century*.
'Martha Lloyd's Cookery Book'. On display at Jane Austen's House, Chawton, Hampshire
Miller, Marc. *The Ancient Art of Cookery*. 1988
Mitchell, Brigette. 'Number 1 Royal Crescent, Bath'. Bath Preservation Trust
Newman, Paul. *Bath*. 1986
Pickford, Ian. *Silver Flatware*. Antique Collectors' Club, Woodbridge, Suffolk, 1988
Powers, Alan. *Shop Fronts*. 1989
Pullar, Phillippa. *Consuming Passions, A History of English Food and Appetite*. 1970
Raffald, Elizabeth. *The Experienced English Housekeeper*. 1976
Sitwell, Edith. *Bath*. 1932
Stead, Jennifer. *Food and Cooking in 18th-Century Britain*. Historic Buildings and Monuments Commission for England, 1985
Tames, Richard. *Josiah Wedgwood 1730–1795*. 1984
Verrall, William. *Cookery Book*. 1759; ed. Ann Haly, Southover Press, Lewes, 1988
Victoria and Albert Museum. *Wedgwood*. 1983
Wallace, Carol McD et al. *Dance, A Very Social History*. The Metropolitan Museum of Art, New York, 1989
*Watson, Winifred. *Jane Austen in London*. C. Mills & Co., Alton, Hampshire, for the Jane Austen Society, 1960
*The Housekeeping Book of Susanna Whatman*. 1987
Woodforde, James. Late Eighteenth-Century Diary, edited by John Beresford as *The Diary of a Country Parson*. 1931

# Acknowledgments

My dear friends Dr Elizabeth Jacobs and Alyce Nash for their unceasing help, advice and encouragement; Andrew Ginger of Colefax and Fowler, who was engaged in restoring Daylesford House; Capt. John Macdonald-Buchanan for his help, patience and courtesy; the staff of the Shakespeare Birthplace Trust; the staff of the Kent County Records Office; the staff of the Hampshire Records Office; the staff of the Northamptonshire Records Office; Lord and Lady Leigh for their kindness in allowing us to photograph Stoneleigh Abbey; Lord and Lady FitzWalter for their kindness in allowing us to photograph Goodnestone Park; George Plumptre for his help with the background of the family of Sir Brook Bridges, and for his hospitality at Rowling House; John B. Sunley for his kindness in allowing us to photograph Godmersham Park; Ian Gow for the benefit of his knowledge of historical interiors; Shelagh Kennedy, curator of The Georgian House, Edinburgh, for her help and hospitality; the staff of the British Museum's Department of Medieval and Later Antiquities; Ed Clark, the V&A picture library; the National Trust for their help and courtesy; Jane Bowie for her expert culinary assistance in preparing eighteenth-century dishes; Jean Bowden, curator of Jane Austen's House, for her great help and patience; Charles Halliday, headmaster, Loretto Junior School, for his kind contribution.

s.w

# Illustration Credits

Courtesy *Antiques Magazine*/photo Will Brown *103 b*; Jane Austen House, Chawton/photo J Butler-Kearney 1, 12, 23, 53; Photo by kind permission of the Jane Austen Society 27 (inset); Bath Preservation Trust, 1 Royal Crescent, Bath 46; Harry R Beard Theatre Collection 171 b; Bodleian Library, Oxford 39; City of Bristol Museum and Art Gallery *31*; City of Bristol Museum and Art Gallery/Bridgeman Art Library *163*; British Museum, London 17, 29, 37, 128, 139 tl, 151, 169 tr, 182, 189, 208 tr; Cottesbrooke Hall. By kind permission of Captain John Macdonald-Buchanan *50/51, 115, 122 b*; Photo *Country Life* 59; Eton College Library. Reproduced by permission of the Provost and Fellows of Eton College 67; Fitzwilliam Museum, Cambridge 41; Garrick Club, London 133; Godmersham Park. By kind permission of Mr J B Sunley *54, 55*; Hampshire County Museum Service 194 t; Photograph reproduced courtesy of *House and Garden*, photographer Simon Brown, interior designer David Easton *126/127*; Kent County Records Office 38, 58, 85, 93, *130/131* (inset), 140, *154* (inset); Museum of London 166 (inset), 169 tl; National Army Museum, London 157 tl, 157 tr; National Gallery of Ireland, Dublin 161; National Portrait Gallery, London 11, 17; National Trust Photographic Library *95 tr*, (John Bethell) *90, 91, 102 b*, (Angelo Hornak) 104 tr, (Rob Matheson) *47 b, 95 tr, 99 b*, (C. Newsholme) 69; Hugh Palmer 2, 6, 8, 26, 27, 30, 43, 46, *47 t, 50/51, 54 tl, 54 tr, 54 b, 55*, 74, 75, *81, 82, 83 t, 83 b, 94, 98, 99 tl, 99 tr, 102, 103 tl, 106 t, 107, 111* (inset), *114, 115, 118 t, 118 b, 119, 122, 123 t, 123 b, 154/155, 158, 166, 167 t, 171, 174, 175 t, 175 b, 202 tl, 202 tr, 203 t, 203 b, 206, 207*; Private Collection 35; Royal Academy of Arts, London *86/87*; Royal Commission of Historical Monuments England 63 t, 63 b; Shelburne Museum, Shelburne, Vermont 141; By kind permission of the Trustees of the Stoneleigh Abbey Preservation Trust *47 t*, 81, *82, 83, 102, 106 t, 107 t, 122 t, 123, 171*; Toledo Museum of Art, Toledo, Ohio, Gift of an Anonymous Donor *42*; Victoria and Albert Museum, London 7, 34, 78, 79 t, 79 b, 97, 104 tl, *130/131, 134, 143, 159 t, 159 b*, 191, 208 l, (Endhoven Collection) 16, 170 (inset); Wallace Collection, London 20; Windsor Castle, Royal Library. © 1990 Her Majesty The Queen 177 tr; Yale Center for British Art, New Haven, Connecticut. Paul Mellon Collection *102/103 t*, 195

R Ackermann, *Repository of Arts* (1800) 129, 167 b, (1809) 9, 19, 142, (1811) 161, (1817) 147; R and J Adam, *Works in Architecture* 1778–1822, 92; J Britton, *The History and Description of Cassiobury Park* 1837, *110/111*; W Felton, *Treatise on Carriages* 1796, 193 tl, 193 tr; E Hastead, *The History and Topographical Survey of the County of Kent* 1799, 49; N Heideloff, *Gallery of Fashion* (1794) 51 (inset), (1801) 137; M C Hill, *Jane Austen, her Homes and her Friends* 1902, 5; T Hope, *Household Furniture and Interior Design* 1809, 112; R Mudie, *Hampshire* 1838, 66; J G Nattes, *Bath* 1806, 179, 186; W H Pyne, *History of the Royal Residences* 1819, 177 tl; Ann Radcliffe, *Mysteries of Udolpho* 1803, 19 (inset); H Repton, *Fragments on the Theory and Practice of Landscape Gardening* 1816, 71 tl, 71 tr, 73; T Rowlandson and A Pugin, *Microcosm of London* 1808, 165, 173; W Smith, *A New and Compendious History of Warwick* 1830, 61; T Wilson, *A Companion to the Ballroom* 1816, 162 (inset).

# Index